YORK
FAMILY TREE

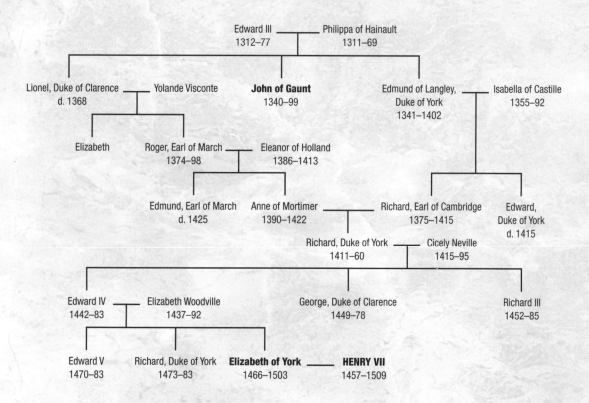

Edward III
1312–77
—
Philippa of Hainault
1311–69

Lionel, Duke of Clarence
d. 1368
—
Yolande Visconte

John of Gaunt
1340–99

Edmund of Langley,
Duke of York
1341–1402
—
Isabella of Castille
1355–92

Elizabeth

Roger, Earl of March
1374–98
—
Eleanor of Holland
1386–1413

Edmund, Earl of March
d. 1425

Anne of Mortimer
1390–1422
—
Richard, Earl of Cambridge
1375–1415

Edward,
Duke of York
d. 1415

Richard, Duke of York
1411–60
—
Cicely Neville
1415–95

Edward IV
1442–83
—
Elizabeth Woodville
1437–92

George, Duke of Clarence
1449–78

Richard III
1452–85

Edward V
1470–83

Richard, Duke of York
1473–83

Elizabeth of York
1466–1503
—
HENRY VII
1457–1509

THE WARS OF THE
ROSES

t vino . . se noftre fouuerain
feigneur . . . e diuard . . . . . art
fur la grace de dieu roy den
gleterre et de france / et feigne
dulande / departift du vais de zellande et

THE WARS OF THE
ROSES

THE CONFLICT THAT INSPIRED
GAME OF THRONES

MARTIN J. DOUGHERTY

METRO BOOKS
New York

METRO BOOKS
New York

An Imprint of Sterling Publishing
1166 Avenue of the Americas
New York, NY 10036

METRO BOOKS and the distinctive Metro Books logo are trademarks
of Sterling Publishing Co., Inc.

Editorial and design by
Amber Books Ltd
74–77 White Lion Street
London N1 9PF
www.amberbooks.co.uk

Project Editor: Sarah Uttridge
Picture Research: Terry Forshaw
Design: Zoë Mellors

ISBN: 978-1-4351-5901-3

For information about custom editions, special sales, and premium and corporate purchases,
please contact Sterling Special Sales at 800-805-5489 or specialsales@sterlingpublishing.com.

Manufactured in China

2 4 6 8 10 9 7 5 3 1

www.sterlingpublishing.com

DISCLAIMER:
The Wars of the Roses is not prepared, authorized, approved or endorsed by any person or entity involved in
the making of Game of Thrones or A Song of Ice and Fire. This is not an official publication and is in no way a
companion or tie-in to any Game of Thrones or A Song of Ice and Fire product.

Contents

• HENRY • II •

INTRODUCTION

In the mid- to late fifteenth century a dispute over the complex matter of the royal succession, combined with the general uncertainty and turbulence of the times, erupted into a power-struggle that wracked England for three decades.

◆

'It was far more complex than a simple clash of two factions'.

At stake were not only power and status but even survival – this was not an era in which the vanquished were treated leniently. Nor was it safe to try to stay out of the game. Powerful lords would use their influence, or outright coercion, to increase their following; refusal to join one side might be taken as membership of the other.

The mid-fifteenth century was a time of great uncertainty and instability. Even as the

The early life of the first Plantagenet king, Henry II of England, was dominated by conflict between his mother Matilda, daughter of Henry I, and Stephen of Blois who held the English crown. Plague (above) claimed many lives during this period.

first flowering of the Renaissance took place in Italy, the private armies of English noble houses warred on one another in the traditional fashion. Plague was a constant threat, as was implication in one of the many plots uncovered at the time. It was not necessary to be guilty in order to be executed; indeed, many individuals were killed simply because they might someday be a rallying point for a rebellion.

The English power-struggle that took place in this era became known as the Wars of the Roses, after the emblems of the two main factions. It was far more complex than a simple clash of two factions, of course. Treachery and disaffection caused some powerful figures to switch sides, and it was not always completely clear who the enemy was.

The Wars of the Roses settled a dynastic question about succession to the English throne

and permitted the Tudor dynasty – which included world-changing figures such as Henry VIII and Elizabeth I – to take power in England. There were also immediate implications for Scotland and France, and wider consequences that would touch even the New World.

This was a critical moment in world history. Columbus would set sail in 1492, just five years after the end of the wars, and soon the settlement of the Americas would begin. The victors of the Wars of the Roses dictated English policies in the settlement of North America and throughout the age of exploration. Closer to home, the Renaissance is generally considered to have reached England in 1487, at the end of the Wars of the Roses. Thus the return of stability to England marked the end of the Middle Ages and the beginning of a new era.

Above: The idea of a 'War of the Roses' originated after the conflict ended, with Renaissance writers. Shakespeare's depiction of lords choosing white or red roses to show factional loyalty in his play *Henry VI Part One* is dramatic invention.

Everything was changing; gunpowder weapons would soon render castles obsolete and the traditional style of warfare, built around armoured knights, would begin its decline. The very way that people viewed themselves and their world was altered forever by the change in thinking that characterized the Renaissance. This was an uncertain time, a

Right: Although the Wars of the Roses were largely between the houses of York and Lancaster, the factions were not tied geographically to those regions to any great extent. Support came from wherever the lords loyal to each faction had their holdings.

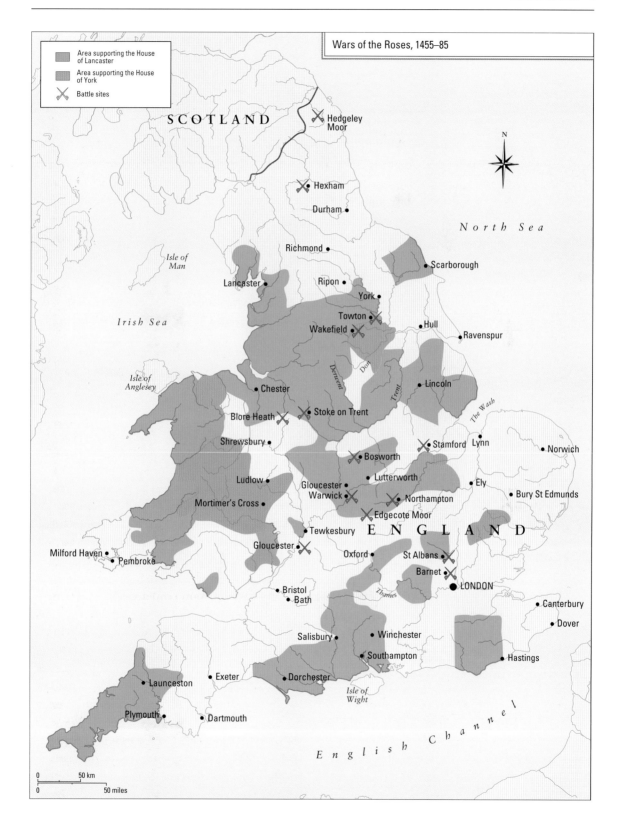

Wars of the Roses, 1455–85

Area supporting the House of Lancaster
Area supporting the House of York
Battle sites

SCOTLAND

Hedgeley Moor

Hexham

Durham

North Sea

Isle of Man

Richmond

Scarborough

Lancaster

Ripon

York

Irish Sea

Towton

Wakefield

Hull

Ravenspur

Derwent

Don

Trent

Lincoln

Isle of Anglesey

Chester

The Wash

Blore Heath

Stoke on Trent

Shrewsbury

Stamford

Lynn

Norwich

Bosworth

Ludlow

Lutterworth

Ely

Gloucester

Warwick

Northampton

Bury St Edmunds

Mortimer's Cross

Edgecote Moor

E N G L A N D

Tewkesbury

Milford Haven

Pembroke

Gloucester

Oxford

St Albans

Barnet

LONDON

Canterbury

Bristol

Bath

Thames

Dover

Salisbury

Winchester

Hastings

Southampton

Launceston

Exeter

Dorchester

Isle of Wight

Plymouth

Dartmouth

E n g l i s h   C h a n n e l

0   50 km

0   50 miles

pivotal moment. The outcome of this last great medieval war would determine the course of European and perhaps even world history for the centuries to come.

Had the Wars of the Roses turned out differently, there would have been no King Henry VIII to break away from the Catholic Church, no Spanish Armada and perhaps no Wars of Religion – or at least they might have had a different outcome. European history would have taken a completely different path, with significant implications for the rest of the world as well.

None of this was known to the people involved as the first conflict broke out. No-one could have predicted three decades of bloody civil war to depose and reinstall an insane king, with one side and then the other in the ascendant. Yet there is more to the Wars of the Roses than the battles. The politics, the murders, the treachery; all played a vital role in determining the outcome of what was no mere dynastic squabble but a battle for control over the future of England.

The Feudal System

Europe in the Middle Ages was governed on a feudal basis. Feudalism was essentially a system of obligations that determined the responsibilities and duties of one social class to another. Feudalism grew up over time, out of the less formal tribal organizations that had previously existed, and was never a formal system of government as such – feudalism is a fairly modern term used to describe a range of broadly similar societies.

In a feudal society, governance was by a military elite, with the king holding the most power and control. Each social stratum had duties to the one above and, in theory at least, responsibilities to those below. Thus the commoners of a village owed their allegiance to a lord of the manor who was in turn responsible for protecting them and settling disputes

between them. This minor lord was usually a knight and owed allegiance to his superior, who might be a baron or higher noble. Loyalty was ultimately to the king, although as time went on this bond became less important than allegiance to the knight's immediate superior.

The king, and any major nobles who were owed allegiance by other noblemen, were liege lords to those who owed them loyalty. The duties required by each party were spelled out in their agreement, and in the case of knights

> '‘No-one could have predicted three decades of bloody civil war to depose and reinstall an insane king, with one side and then the other in the ascendant’.

and higher nobles usually included military service. Commoners also owed a duty of military service to their lord if he chose to call them. A subordinate might be given a specific task, such as to be custodian of a royal castle without taking ownership of it, or might simply be on call when needed for military service and free to pursue his own interests the rest of the time. A great nobleman (including the monarch) might maintain several or even many knights and professional soldiers at his own expense, but there was a limit to how many could be supported by even the richest nobleman.

Most of the military elite were supported by granting them land as vassals. The term vassal applies to anyone who has entered into an agreement of feudal loyalty, but is often used in the context of landed vassals, i.e. those that have been granted lands in return for their service. Land could be held under various forms of tenure ranging from what was essentially temporary use in return for service to hereditary ownership.

A land grant, or any source of revenue such as rights of taxation or a position of power that created an income, was termed a fief (or formerly a fee). A manor, producing enough revenue to support a knight, was a typical fief. Depending on the terms of enfeoffment in place, the lord of a manor might be free to make as much money as he could from his holdings. This could be very lucrative in the case where a fief was held in return for a fixed rent or for military service. This was typically for 40 days a year. Those that wished to be exempted from military service were sometimes permitted to pay scutage ('shield money'), essentially a fee in return for

exemption from other duties. Scutage could allow a nobleman to use surplus revenue from his holdings to gain exemption from service, keeping the remainder for himself. Other forms of enfeoffment, such as those connected with the clergy, also did not require military service although other duties had to be fulfilled..

Granting lands to vassals allowed them to take responsibility for running them rather than the monarch trying to micromanage his whole country, and allowed fighting men

Below: In the bastard feudal society of the 1400s, the king no longer held absolute authority. Great lords and Church officials also wielded huge influence, creating endless political intrigues, plots and bargains among those close to the throne.

to be supported at a local level when not on campaign. During peacetime they would – in theory – contribute to stability and the rule of law in their home area without draining central resources. This was an age when standing armies were not maintained, other than the household forces of the nobility. At need, a force was assembled by calling knights to service, and they would bring with them their own soldiers and any additional personnel recruited by levying them from the common population.

However, granting land allowed vassals to become increasingly rich and powerful if their holdings were well (or, in the short term at least, rapaciously) managed. Some fiefs reverted to the king upon the vassal's death but many were hereditary, creating a need to determine

> 'Some fiefs reverted to the king upon the vassal's death but many were hereditary, creating a need to determine who they would pass to'.

who they would pass to. This was usually the eldest male heir, but more distant relatives might inherit if there was none. Marriages also caused holdings to pass from one family to another, which could result in the fragmentation or consolidation of fiefs.

Consolidation or acquisition of additional fiefdoms permitted the greater nobility to

Below: As heir to Henry III, the young Edward I played an important part in the Second Barons' War. Once enthroned, he set about implementing social and legal reforms that addressed some of the causes of the conflict.

increase their wealth and status, which gradually led to the emergence of great noble houses wielding enormous power. An alliance of such nobles – or just a single house in some cases – could rival the king in terms of political and military power, which had implications for the governance of the kingdom.

Governance of a realm increasingly became a balancing act, in which the king needed the support of the great nobles rather than being able to simply dictate to them. So long as the king had enough supporters at any given time, he could proceed as he wished. However, this support was a two-way street and rulership became increasingly about compromise. Indeed, at times the king might be ineffectual, his power eclipsed by that of the great nobility. However, the office of the king still held a lot of influence; generally speaking, lip-service at least had to be paid to loyalty and obedience.

In this environment, politics and disputes among the great nobility could influence national policy, and private wars between nobles could rage out of control. A strong king, with solid support, could bring those of his nobles who required it to order but there was always a price for support. As the great nobility became increasingly powerful the king went from absolute ruler to just another powerful player in a very dangerous game.

As time went on, the nature of feudalism

Above: Edward I is primarily famous for his campaigns in Scotland, which earned him the nickname 'Hammer of the Scots'. He was very much a warrior king, fighting in Wales, Scotland and on crusade as well as against rebels in England.

changed. Rather than everyone owing allegiance to the king, many people at lower levels considered their first loyalty was to their liege lord. This created greater factionalisation and increased the power of the nobility relative to the king. At the same time, there was a shift in the way that military service to the crown was managed. During the reign of Edward I (1272–1307), the practice of direct service when called was replaced with a system based on money.

The new system called for a financial contribution paid by each social stratum to their liege lord rather than fighting when called upon to do so. If military service was required then the liege would pay for it. Thus in a quiet year money could be spent on other projects

or put into a war chest for future need. Large forces could be raised when required by hiring professional troops as well as paying vassals for their military contribution to the conflict. This new system has been termed 'bastard feudalism'. Under bastard feudalism, the nobility could afford to maintain bodies of troops under arms on a permanent basis if they chose, although these forces would be small. In times of peace this retinue was used to guard holdings, to deal with trouble and to act as a bodyguard as well as being a status symbol. When there was a conflict with another lord or an overseas campaign, the retinue would be expanded with additional men.

The increasing power of the great nobility under bastard feudalism was one factor in ensuring that the Wars of the Roses era was so bloody. Powerful nobles with their own private armies could engage in conflict with one another, and it might be that the king lacked the capability

Opposite: The production of a male heir was an important factor in the stability of a kingdom. Edward I had three sons before the boy who would reign as Edward II was born; two died before his birth and one just after.

to stop them. He might also choose not to, allowing his nobles to pursue their own agendas either because he supported them or because he wanted their support in some other matter. Arguably, the weakening of the crown's position relative to the great nobility was one of the main factors in permitting the Wars of the Roses to take place.

> 'Primogeniture and the inheritance of an intact position ensured that holdings remained concentrated and power was not diluted'.

Inheritance and Succession

The question of who inherited a fief when the current holder died was an important one; the question of who took the throne upon the death of the king even more so. If the fief was not hereditary then it reverted to the control of the holder's liege lord, who could then reassign it. Hereditary holdings were generally inherited by the eldest male child of the holder.

This form of inheritance, termed male primogeniture, worked well enough when there was a male child to inherit, although it meant that younger sons might receive very little. It was generally not thought desirable to divide

Right: John of Gaunt was the first Duke of Lancaster. His son, King Henry IV, was a legitimate child. Other children, with the family name of Beaufort, were born out of wedlock but later legitimized, creating an ambiguous situation regarding inheritance.

holdings evenly among multiple inheritors, not least because this might subdivide the family's holdings to the point where none of the fiefs was sufficient to maintain their previous social status. In the case of a kingdom, subdivision among the heirs was unlikely to be a successful measure.

Primogeniture and the inheritance of an intact position ensured that holdings remained concentrated and power was not diluted, though it did at times result in rivalries and bitterness between siblings. Younger sons might be granted a subordinate position or have fiefs of their own, and in addition the royal family and the greater noble houses would commonly grant a lesser fiefdom or title to younger sons. Among such grants, termed appanages, were the duchies of Lancaster and York. These were created for the younger sons of Edward III, granting them wealth and status appropriate to their station as brothers of the king. Most appanages were less substantial, but they did ensure that the younger sons and their families remained part of the nobility or at least the gentry.

A fief or position might pass to a younger son if his elder brother died before producing any male heirs, but if not, then the younger son and his descendants would form what was termed a cadet branch of the noble house. A cadet branch was out of the line of succession for the main branch's holdings, but would pass its own down the generations by the same mechanism and might increase its power by marriage or other means.

In the event that a royal line or noble house was without heirs, eligibility to inherit could be traced back up the family tree and then down the senior cadet branch of the family until a suitable candidate was found. This ensured that there were always several individuals with a valid blood claim to the throne, albeit a distant one, and that could be a mixed blessing for them. Plots might form around such an individual, whether or not they wanted any part of it, and at times distant relatives were executed to ensure that they did not threaten the current claimant to the throne's position.

The situation was made more complicated by the fact that lineage could be traced different ways. Agnatic primogeniture considered only descendants of the male line unless there were none, in which case a female relative might inherit. This excluded otherwise eligible candidates who were descended through a female ancestor and might result in succession passing to a more distant relative.

The availability of an adult male heir was thus highly important for stability. Where one existed, the process of installing a new king or the head of a great noble family was relatively straightforward. Where the succession was less clear, or the heir was a young child, things were a lot more complicated. Blood claims to a position could be made by many individuals, and some great nobles might decide that it was not in their best interests to accept the strongest blood claim.

Creative interpretation of blood claims was also a factor, with disputes over what factors made a claim ineligible or stronger than another. Many candidates had more than one claim, being related to the royal line by different paths, or had some factor that their opponents might consider barred them from succession. Negotiation, influence and the threat of force were all brought into play when negotiating a succession, and when that failed open warfare was always an option.

England and France in the Late Middle Ages

The concept of nationhood as we know it today did not exist in the Middle Ages. States such as England or France did exist, but the way they were defined was somewhat different. Rather than being a formally defined nation with borders and territories delineated by international treaties, a state such as England or France was partly a cultural concept, partly a matter of tradition and partly a question of allegiance.

Exactly what regions constituted France (or England) varied over time, and was also a matter of viewpoint. Whilst it is relatively easy to draw a map with neat borders running along mountain ranges, rivers and coasts, and to claim that the areas within are part of a given state, the reality at any time was more complex. It might

> 'The name Plantagenet, meaning "Sprig of Broom", referring to the crest of the Angevin dynasty, was initially a nickname'.

be reasonable to define England or France as the areas owing allegiance to the crown of that state, either directly or through a great noble house. Even here, there are questions about the reality of this allegiance. Some areas claimed by the French crown were entirely beyond its control for most of the Middle Ages. Other areas were indisputably French but were under the control of nobles whose loyalty to the French throne was slight. In some cases, territories within France were held by noble houses loyal to a foreign king.

Significant parts of France were held by English nobles whose allegiance was, of course, to the King of England. This was perhaps an inevitable consequence of the existence of noble houses; powerful families intermarried and linked together holdings that might be part of entirely different realms. This created a situation where an individual might be a French count

or duke and also the king of England. Such an individual might be received by the French king as a fellow monarch on some occasions, and on others would be expected to pay homage as a subordinate.

The situation in France and England owed much to the life and actions of Henry II of England (reigned 1154–89). Known as Henry Plantagenet, first of that family name, Henry was the child of Matilda, daughter of the English King Henry I, and Geoffrey of Anjou. The name Plantagenet, meaning 'Sprig of Broom', referring to the crest of the Angevin dynasty, was initially a nickname; Henry was a member of the Angevin dynasty and was Duke of Normandy, Count of Anjou and had several other French titles as well. He married Eleanor of Aquitaine and added that duchy to

Right: The possession of territories in France created a situation whereby the English king was also a French duke and therefore subordinate to the king of France. Attempts to force the king of England to humble himself before a rival monarch greatly increased friction.

his family's list of territories. Thus the king of England had claims to large parts of France, but these were not English territories as such – at least, not according to the French king. Henry II took the throne of England after a long period of instability and civil war, but was not content with re-establishing the rule of the English throne. He campaigned in Wales, Ireland and France, expanding his territories into what is often termed the Angevin Empire.

The Angevin Empire shrank rapidly after Henry's death. His son, Richard I ('The Lionheart') spent more time in Aquitaine or on crusade than in England, and gave little thought

---

'The king of England had claims to large parts of France, but these were not English territories as such – at least not according to the French king'.

---

to the management of any of his holdings. Upon his death in 1199 the crown passed to his brother John, whose reign was sufficiently disastrous that there will never be another English king of the same name.

John's kingship started out well enough. Angevin holdings in France were recognized by the French king, Philip II, in 1200. However, war between England and France soon broke out, and most of the Angevin lands in northern France were lost. John tried to regain them for several years, unsuccessfully, and was then

Left: Already holding large territories in France as a member of the Angevin dynasty, Henry II of England gained the Duchy of Aquitaine by marrying Eleanor of Aquitaine. This represented a peak in England's fortunes; much of Henry's 'Angevin Empire' would soon be lost.

forced to confront a major rebellion in England. This rebellion was significant for many reasons; not least because it resulted in the Magna Carta, a charter which limited the ability of the English king to do as he pleased. Henceforth, even the king could not imprison or harm a free man without some legal reason for doing so. It may seem obvious today that the king's will should be subordinate to the law, but at that time it was a new concept.

The Magna Carta

The Magna Carta was the first legally binding document to be imposed upon the English king by his subjects, and illustrates the changing nature of English feudalism. No longer an absolute monarch, the king was forced to accept an agreement with his senior nobles. Among its clauses, Magna Carta included the provision that the great nobles could, acting in concert, overrule the king and even take possession of his castles if he did not comply with the charter. Of course, John did not comply with the charter; he renounced it as soon as he was able and was supported by the Pope in doing so. The charter outlived him however; he died in 1216 and was succeeded by his nine-year-old son Henry who accepted the provisions of the Magna Carta and thus ensured that it remained as a foundation of British law.

As a young man, Henry III attempted to regain his lands in France, which ended in disaster, and tried again in 1242. In 1259 a treaty was agreed with France whereby Henry gave up all claims to his French lands except Gascony, and in return his position there was recognized. This agreement was not Henry's own doing; the senior nobles of England had essentially taken power the year before and kept the king as a figurehead.

Royal control was re-established in England after the Second Barons' War of 1264–7. The first was fought against King John and established limitations on Royal power; the second resulted in further reforms and the giving of a voice in government to non-nobles. Henry and his son Edward were captured and imprisoned, although Henry kept his position as king. This period as a figurehead or puppet ended when Edward escaped and defeated the baronial forces in battle.

The reign of Edward I began upon the death of his father in 1272 and was characterized mainly by wars in Wales and Scotland as well as attempts to reform English law. Edward was something of a peacemaker in Europe, although this was mainly in the hope of aligning support behind his plan for a vast and unified crusade. He was also effective in controlling the growing power of the great nobility in England.

In one of many attempts to reconcile differences between England and France, Edward I's son and successor, Edward II, married Isabella, daughter of the French king Philip IV, in 1308. This involved some difficult negotiations, including difficulties over the

> 'Edward was something of a peacemaker in Europe, although this was mainly in the hope of aligning support behind his plan for a vast and unified crusade'.

requirement that Edward pay homage to Philip as one of his vassals rather than interacting as fellow monarchs. Despite efforts to prevent it, war between England and France erupted once more in 1324. As usual, the English possessions in Gascony were a flashpoint; the new French king Charles IV demanded that his vassal, Edward, Duke of Gascony, come to Paris and pay homage. Edward, king of England, decided not to comply. Tensions escalated, resulting in an invasion of Gascony.

In an attempt to end the conflict, Edward II granted Gascony to his son, who was also called Edward, and sent him to Paris to give homage

Right: The Second Barons' War took place from 1264–1267, putting a group of powerful lords under the leadership of Simon de Montfort against Henry III of England. Henry was captured and for a time ruled as a figurehead controlled by his enemies.

to the French king. Edward II's wife, Isabella, was also in Paris and did much to facilitate the settlement, although her relations with her husband changed considerably around this time. After concluding a peace with France, Isabella began accumulating support for a military campaign against her husband's realm.

Edward II's reign ended in disaster. His policies and alliances with unpopular lords had alienated much of the country, and as Isabella and her son landed in England, the population of London rose up against their king. Edward fled, hoping to raise an army in Wales or perhaps escape to Ireland. He was captured and agreed to abdicate in favour of his son, who took the throne as Edward III in 1327.

Edward III reversed many of his father's unpopular policies and was successful in restoring the authority of the crown despite starting his reign as a figurehead for his mother and her lover, Roger Mortimer. He increased English military capability, basing his tactics around the combined-arms cooperation of armoured cavalry with longbowmen. This system proved to serve well in wars with Scotland, and in due course was employed against France.

Below: Edward II of England married Isabella of France in January 1308. Isabella was the daughter of King Philip IV of France, giving the descendants of Edward and Isabella a claim to the French throne that would cause great friction in the years to come.

Right: Edward II and Isabella of France were married at Boulogne-sur-Mer in January 1308, after which Isabella journeyed to England to be crowned as Queen Consort in February. Their partnership was initially successful, but eventually ended in open military conflict.

In 1328 Charles IV of France died. He had no obvious heirs, but there were potential claimants to the throne. Among them was Edward III, king of England. He asserted his claim to the throne as the son of Isabella, Charles' sister. This was not to the liking of the French nobility, who cited Salic law to bar Edward's claim. Salic law had governed French matters of succession since the time of the Frankish kingdoms, basing inheritance on agnatic primogeniture, meaning that the throne would pass to the eldest male child of the monarch, and if there were none then to the closest male relative. Since Edward's claim was by way of the female line, he was ruled to be completely outside the line of succession. Instead, Charles' cousin Philip was chosen to succeed him.

Not only was he refused the French throne but, as Duke of Aquitaine, Edward III was required to pay homage to the new French king. He did so in 1329, but decided to wear his own crown whilst doing so. This did little to improve relations, and as tensions escalated the French king decided to strip the Duke of Aquitaine of his lands. In response Edward challenged the right of Philip IV to be king of France and, despite the fact that many in France considered his reluctant homage in 1329 to be a withdrawal of his claims to the French throne, began to press his own claim again. Edward's attempt to land his army in France in 1340 was resisted, leading to

the naval Battle of Sluys which was a decisive English victory. Sluys gave England control over the English Channel, enabling the English kings to mount expeditions whenever they chose and reducing the danger of a French invasion.

After intervening in the Breton War of Succession, Edward launched a major expedition into France in 1346. The campaign was conducted as a raid in force, causing political and economic damage by pillaging rather than attempting to take and hold political centres such as cities and castles. Marching towards the Low Countries from Caen,

Edward's army was forced south by the need to find an unimpeded crossing of the Seine. This took it close to Paris, but Edward did not besiege the city. Instead he continued his march northeastwards with the French army in pursuit.

Edward eventually made a stand, resulting in the Battle of Crécy. Here, he used a combined-arms approach to battle contrasting with the French reliance on heavily armoured cavalry. Dismounted knights and footsoldiers provided protection for longbowmen, who were able to break up disorganized French charges. The result was a decisive victory for England, leading to the capture of the port of Calais.

This opening act of what would become known as the Hundred Years War was followed

> 'Dismounted knights and footsoldiers provided protection for longbowmen, who were able to break up several gallant but disorganized French charges'.

by a period of disruption caused largely by the Black Death. It was not until 1356 that the English were able to undertake further operations in France. This time they used Gascony as a base and were able to capture King John II of France at the Battle of Poitiers. The resulting regency in France was weak, and the English took advantage of internal troubles to launch another invasion.

The English goal was to capture Reims, the traditional site of French coronations.

Left: At the Battle of Crécy in 1346, Edward III of England made use of rising ground to weaken the French charges. Longbowmen protected by dismounted men-at-arms prevented the French from breaking the outnumbered English line.

This did not prove possible; the city resisted a five-week siege, after which the English army marched on Paris where it was again repulsed. In a negotiated settlement, Edward accepted an enlargement of his Aquitanian holdings in return for renouncing his claim to the French throne and to other regions including Anjou and Normandy.

After a period of peace, France and England found themselves backing rival claimants for the throne of Castile, and the situation deteriorated again until in 1369 England and France were once more at war. Although he reasserted his claim to the French throne, there was little that Edward III could do. His own health was failing and his son (also called Edward but generally known as the Black Prince) was ill. Both died within a year of one another, and in 1377 the son of Edward the Black Prince took the throne of England as Richard II. He was at that time 10 years old.

During King Richard's boyhood, his reign was heavily influenced by a group of favourites at court. This was challenged in 1387 by a group of noblemen calling themselves the Lords Appellant, who gained control over the young king and the country for the next two years. Richard, who was becoming increasingly unpopular, managed to come to an

Opposite: Richard II became King of England at the age of 10, which placed power in the hands of a council of regents. His subsequent seizure of his own power as king led to a period known as his 'tyranny'.

Below: Stripped of his inheritance by Richard II, Henry Bolingbroke returned from exile and deposed Richard, taking the throne as Henry IV. His reign was plagued by internal conflict, some of which spilled over into the Wars of the Roses period.

accommodation with the Lords Appellant that lasted from 1389 to 1397, at which point he took decisive action to restore his power.

Richard's subsequent actions became known as his 'tyranny'. He stripped Henry Bolingbroke, son of Richard's uncle John of Gaunt, of his inheritance. Henry was in exile at the time, but now returned and successfully deposed Richard. In 1400 Richard II died whilst imprisoned, under somewhat mysterious circumstances.

Henry VI of England

Henry Bolingbroke was crowned Henry IV of England, and had intended to resume the ongoing wars with France. Instead he became embroiled in internal troubles, with rebellions ongoing in Wales and conflict with Scotland. The latter led to the powerful Percy family of northern England entering into open conflict with Henry.

Meanwhile, France was also dealing with internal power-struggles, resulting in a lull in the wars. This came to an end after Henry IV died and his son took the English throne as Henry V. Within months of his coronation in 1413, Henry V was planning how to exploit French weakness. He made territorial demands that were not acceptable to the French crown and when they were inevitably rejected, he began planning an offensive into France.

1

FOUNDATIONS OF THE WARS OF THE ROSES

At the time of Henry V's coronation in 1413, France was weak, creating a good opportunity for Henry to press his claim to the French crown as a descendant of Edward III. Resistance to an invasion was likely to be slow in developing, disorganized and perhaps half-hearted.

◆

'He became known for a time as Charles the Beloved'.

The French king was unpopular, the kingdom was financially embarrassed and it was even possible that some French nobles would accept or at least not oppose an English bid for the throne.

The French king, Charles VI, had taken the throne in 1380 at the age of 11. He could not legally wield power at this age so four of his

The great English victory won by Henry V at Agincourt in 1415 may have prompted the French king Charles VI into a fit of madness; a trait passed on to his descendants. The coronation of Henry V (above) was held at Westminster Abbey in 1413.

uncles – all of course great nobles in their own right, and with agendas of their own – were to govern the country until Charles came of age at 14. In the event it was actually several more years before Charles was able to assert himself, and by this time his regents had created several serious problems.

Charles' four uncles put their own interests foremost, spending royal money on projects of their own or to block the manoeuvres of the others. Increased taxation to pay for all this infighting created unrest and even revolts, until finally Charles took power in his own right and began to restore matters. He was sufficiently successful that he became known for a time as Charles the Beloved, largely as a result of a brief period of prosperity created by his policies.

Mental illness ran in the family of Charles the Beloved, and in 1392 it manifested itself for the first time. Whilst on the way to Brittany, Charles suddenly lapsed into violent insanity and killed members of his own escort before he could be restrained. Further episodes followed, in which he would attack anyone nearby or flee in terror from unseen assailants. Between bouts of insanity he was rational, but not capable of good governance. This led to a

Below: In 1392, Charles VI of France suddenly turned on his escort and attacked them. His subsequent bouts of insanity gained him the nickname 'Charles the Mad'. This tendency to madness was passed to his descendants including Henry VI of England.

new set of power-struggles in France, which gradually became a civil war between the Duke of Burgundy and a faction named for Bernard, Duke of Armagnac.

With France in such turmoil, Henry V considered he had an excellent opportunity to make territorial gains. His plans were initially opposed by Parliament, which preferred negotiation, but by early 1415 Parliament had agreed to sanction war with France.

Plots against Henry

Although he eventually obtained the reluctant support of Parliament for his invasion of France, Henry faced internal troubles that had to be

'Whilst on the way to Brittany, Charles suddenly lapsed into violent insanity and killed members of his own escort before he could be restrained'.

dealt with before he could launch a foreign expedition. He had been generally successful in building support among the nobility of England, restoring the estates and titles of those who had lost them during his father's reign. His first two years on the throne were not without their troubles, however.

One challenge came from the religious movement known as the Lollards, who were opposed to various features of the Catholic Church. The Lollards believed religion to be very much a personal matter, with Scripture accessible to all who could read it in English. They also were at odds with the idea of a politically powerful and wealthy Church, believing that religion should be separated from politics. These dangerous ideas ran contrary to the accepted order of things, although some powerful noblemen supported the movement.

Among these was John of Gaunt, Duke of Lancaster and grandfather of Henry V of England. Other noblemen embraced the concepts of Lollardy but tended to be discreet about their support for what was at times considered heresy. The Lollard movement was seen as a serious threat to the existing social structure; sufficiently so that John of Gaunt's son, Henry IV, passed laws that prohibited some aspects of Lollard practice such as translating the Bible into English, and also authorized the practice of punishing heresy by burning at the stake, which was continued into Henry V's reign. Indeed, just before his coronation in 1413, his friend John Oldcastle was accused of heresy as a member of the Lollard movement. Henry V tried to persuade Oldcastle to relent of his heretical beliefs, but he would not do so.

This placed Henry in a difficult position. He did not want to act against his friend, but Lollardy was a serious threat to stability in his kingdom and Henry needed the support of the Church as well as the great nobility. He permitted proceedings against Oldcastle to go ahead, but granted him a reprieve whilst he tried further persuasion. These half-measures worked against Henry. Oldcastle escaped from the Tower of London and led a Lollard insurrection against the crown. His plan was to kidnap King Henry and set himself up as Regent, which would allow religious and social reforms to be pushed through. Henry was warned of the plot, which came to nothing, but Oldcastle continued to be a nuisance until 1417. He was involved in various plots during the next few years, including the Southampton Plot. Most of these intrigues achieved little, and eventually Oldcastle was captured. He was put to death in

Opposite: Henry Bolingbroke had a blood claim to the throne as a son of John of Gaunt. However, his bid to take it was successful more due to Richard II's increasing unpopularity than the legality of Henry's claim.

1417, though sources vary on whether he was burned as a heretic or was hanged and then burned. Either way, Henry V was forced to have his old friend put to death in a horrible manner for the sake of stability in his kingdom.

Edmund Mortimer's Claim

A more persistent problem was the claim of Edmund Mortimer to the English throne. Mortimer was Earl of March, and descended from the second son of Edward III. This gave him a better claim than Henry V, who was descended from Edward's third son. Mortimer

'Oldcastle was captured. He was put to death in 1417, though sources vary on whether he was burned as a heretic or was hanged then burned.'

and his father had also been heirs presumptive to Richard II. Essentially this meant that unless Richard produced a son who would be his heir, the Mortimers would inherit the throne of England. That changed when Richard II was deposed by his cousin Henry Bolingbroke (Henry IV).

In 1403 the powerful Percy family, Earls of Northumberland, had revolted and attempted to overthrow Henry IV. Their bid was unsuccessful, with some of the ringleaders captured and sentenced to death by hanging, drawing and quartering. The Earl of Northumberland managed to escape to Scotland and raise another force. A second attempt in 1405 was also defeated. This time the rebel leaders were tried under irregular circumstances before being sentenced to death by beheading. A third rising in 1408 was also soundly defeated. Instrumental in putting down these rebellions was the young man who would become Henry V.

At the time of the 1403–8 rebellions, rumours persisted that Richard II was still alive, perhaps in exile at the court of Scotland. A successful uprising could put him back on the throne in place of Henry IV who had deposed him. Alternatively, Edmund Mortimer, Earl of March, was an excellent candidate to replace Henry. The risings failed, of course, but the

> 'The intent was to kill Henry and his brothers at Southampton whilst final preparations were being made to invade France'.

intrigues continued after Henry IV died and his son Henry V took the throne.

Edmund Mortimer and his brother Roger had spent several years under close supervision during the reign of Henry IV, with the young Henry V as his guardian for much of this time. Edmund and Henry were of similar ages, and despite whatever resentment Edmund might have harboured about no longer being heir to the throne, he became a loyal supporter of Henry. As one of his first acts as king, Henry V freed the Mortimer brothers and inducted them into the Order of the Bath. Mortimer was among those who attended the Parliament in 1415 that agreed to war against France, and subsequently took part in Henry's campaign. In the meantime, he became aware of a conspiracy that had developed.

Known variously as the Cambridge Plot or the Southampton Plot, the plan was led by the Earl of Cambridge. The intent was to kill Henry and his brothers at Southampton whilst final preparations were being made to invade France, and to install Mortimer as king. However, Mortimer revealed the plot to Henry and the leaders were arrested. Mortimer took part in the investigation that condemned the Earl of Cambridge – Mortimer's brother-in-law – to death.

Mortimer subsequently accompanied Henry to France but returned after contracting dysentery at the siege of Harfleur. He rejoined later campaigns and played a prominent role in the coronation of Henry's French bride, Catherine of Valois. His strong blood claim to the throne could have made him or his descendants a threat had another plot formed around the family, but Mortimer died without issue. Upon his death in 1425 his estate and titles passed to Richard, Duke of York.

Henry's Campaigns in France

Whilst the Southampton Plot was unfolding, Henry V raised an army for his invasion of France. His force landed during August 1415, marching quickly to besiege the port of Harfleur. The siege was made famous by Shakespeare's play, and was undertaken to secure a line of communication back to England. Possession of a port would allow supplies and reinforcements to be brought in without undue difficulty, and until this was assured Henry's army was in a difficult position without the prospect of resupply or retreat if seriously threatened.

The siege followed a fairly conventional pattern for the era. After surrounding the city to cut it off, the English set up a battery of cannon, covered by archers, and created breaches in the walls. The defenders offered an accommodation whereby the city would be surrendered if not

Opposite: Edmund Mortimer was a potential threat to Henry IV, and thus was arrested and closely watched. He became a good friend and supporter of his captor, the young Henry V, and was released as soon as Henry V became king.

relieved by 23 September. No French army had arrived during the month-long siege, other than some local reinforcements rushed in as soon as the English arrived, so Harfleur duly surrendered. Although he had captured his first objective, Henry was not in a good position. An outbreak of dysentery among his troops, added to casualties from the siege, reduced his army to the point where he could not effectively continue the campaign. A withdrawal to England was not acceptable as it would make the campaign look like a failure, so Henry resolved to march to Calais.

Henry's plan was to undertake a variant on the well-established tactic of the chevauchée. As the name suggests, this was normally a fast-moving mounted raid, but Henry intended to accomplish much the same level of destruction by marching an army mostly composed of footsoldiers through enemy territory. His army would destroy whatever his men could not carry off, weakening the French economically as well as politically by demonstrating the inability of the French king to defend his territory.

The raid would allow Henry's depleted army to accomplish enough for the campaign to be considered a success, but reaching Calais required crossing the River Somme, which in turn meant pushing south until a viable crossing was found. The French, meanwhile, had been gathering an army and now moved to engage the

Opposite: A dramatic but fanciful representation of the battle of Agincourt. Good choice of terrain on Henry V's part channelled the superior French force into a killing ground where the longbows of Henry's army were devastatingly effective.

'A withdrawal to England was not acceptable as it would make the campaign look like a failure, so Henry resolved to march to Calais'.

Left: The longbow was crucial to English tactics, enabling English forces to strike at a distance. Enemies who managed to get close enough were met with rows of emplaced stakes and a force of dismounted men-at-arms who protected the archers.

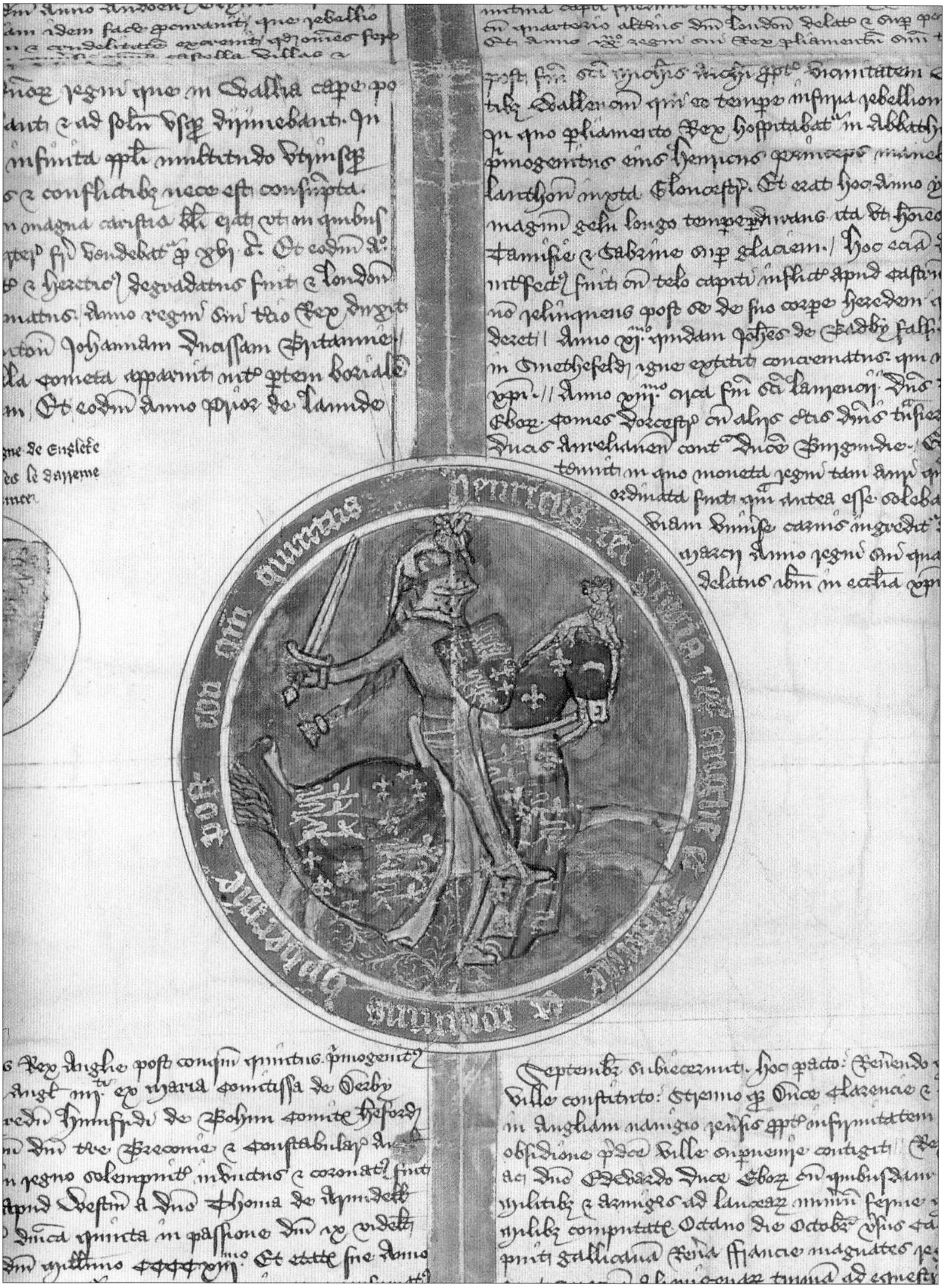

Opposite: Like all other aspects of the monarchy, the royal seal was rather grand. It signified that a document had the force of law and, perhaps more importantly, represented the will of a king who would be prepared to fight to enforce it.

English invaders. They succeeded in positioning themselves between Henry's army and its destination. Unable to break contact or get past the French host, Henry was forced to fight near Agincourt in north-eastern France.

The French fielded around 20,000 troops under Charles d'Albret, Constable of France. Strategically, they had enormous advantages over the English, who were badly outnumbered,

'Henry ordered prisoners already taken to be put to death in case they took arms once again. This was not his only merciless act as a commander'.

short of supplies and suffering from disease. Most of the 6000 or so English soldiers on the field were longbowmen, many of whom were so badly affected by dysentery that they fought without trousers. The English could field around 750 armoured men-at-arms; the French around 7000 on horseback plus about twice that number on foot. The French host was thus more mobile as well as being more combat-effective, and could afford to simply stand between Henry and his objective while the English ran out of supplies. However, when the English army moved forward into longbow range and began peppering their front lines with arrows, the French decided to attack.

The French cavalry were channelled into a fairly narrow frontage by woods on each side of the battlefield, creating ideal conditions for the English archers. Those that reached the English line, struggling over downed comrades and through ground that was quickly churned up into mud, were engaged by the Englishmen-at-arms. Despite being very hard pressed, Henry's outnumbered army was able to repulse the French attacks and resume its march to Calais. However, things looked bad enough at one point that Henry ordered prisoners already taken to be put to death in case they took up arms once again. This was not his only merciless act as a commander, although it was for pragmatic reasons rather than simple spite.

Victory at Agincourt did not change the strategic picture all that much, although Harfleur remained in English hands despite an attempt to retake it in 1416. From 1417 onward Henry was successful in his renewed campaign, besieging Rouen until its surrender in 1419. Here again, Henry showed his ruthlessness in executing many of those who had opposed him. He also refused to allow passage to women and children sent out of the starving city, consigning them to a slow death between the city walls and the siege lines.

The Treaty of Troyes
In late 1419, Henry's army reached Paris, where the court was crippled by political infighting and the insanity of Charles VI – who was no longer known as 'the Beloved' but was now 'Charles the Mad'. With no real chance of successful resistance, Charles was forced to sign the Treaty of Troyes, which named Henry of England as regent of France and Charles' heir. Henry married Catherine, Charles' daughter, in 1420. She bore him a son, who would be Henry VI of England and would display his grandfather's tendency towards madness.

Henry V continued to campaign in France in 1421–2, but was never crowned King of France. He died of disease on campaign just two months before Charles VI died, leaving his infant son as king of England and creating a power vacuum that ultimately led to the Wars of the Roses.

The Early Life of Richard of York

Richard Plantagenet was born in 1411 and became Duke of York upon the death of his uncle, Edward, at the Battle of Agincourt. He was at the time four years old, and was placed under the protection of Ralph Neville, Duke of Westmoreland. In the same year Richard's father, Richard of Conisburgh, Earl of Cambridge, was executed for his part in the Southampton Plot.

Richard, now Richard of York, was the great-grandson of Edward III. He was somewhat removed from the direct line of succession – his grandfather, Edmund of Langley, was the fourth son of the king, and Richard's father was a second son. Nevertheless, Richard had a blood claim to the throne if closer heirs did not exist. On his mother's side, Richard was a nephew of Roger Mortimer, the Earl of March. Mortimer was also descended from Edward III by way of Lionel of Antwerp, second surviving son of Edward III. He was thus more closely related to Edward III than Henry VI was, since Henry's line ran through Edward's third son.

It was a harsh fact of life in the Middle Ages that a close relative might be executed, and his heirs then expected to interact with the man

Below: Richard, Duke of York, was a successful military commander and was popular in England. Until the birth of the future Henry VI, Richard was the heir presumptive to the English throne. He served as regent during Henry VI's early madness.

who had ordered it or even to serve him in an important capacity. So it was with Richard of York; he was part of the social system that Henry V headed, and thus a servant of the crown. Richard's father died for plotting to murder the king but his uncle was killed fighting loyally alongside Henry at Agincourt.

The involvement of one family member in treason could be disastrous for all their relatives, but it was more common for the individual to be punished and his family to continue to hold their lands and positions. A vindictive king, or one who wanted to transfer power and wealth to his favourites, might use the crimes of one family member as an excuse to strip away lands or titles, but too much of this could weaken the social structure that supported the king. Thus, although much of the land held by Richard's uncle reverted to the crown according to the terms under which it was granted, Richard retained enough to make him extremely powerful and wealthy once he reached adulthood, and thus he was an important member of the court. His status was further increased when he inherited the lands of the Earl of March in 1425.

Richard of York was at this time the most powerful man in England after the king, and

Below: John Beaufort, Duke of Somerset, was a royal favourite but a poor military commander. His campaign in Gascony brought only failure and disgrace, and had the side-effect of increasing the disaffection felt by Richard of York.

therefore potentially a threat. One way to keep him out of trouble was to send him overseas on an important mission, and in 1436 he was given the task of protecting English holdings in France. In due course this led to him being appointed Lieutenant of France. This was a position of great trust and responsibility; Richard was the king's representative on the Continent, wielding enormous military and political power in his name. He also had to assume some financial responsibility for the forces under his command, and contributed large sums to the maintenance of his army. This was nothing new; his predecessor the Duke of Bedford had done the same.

Retaining English Holdings

Nevertheless, Richard's military resources were stretched thin trying to retain English holdings in northern France. The Treaty of Arras, signed in 1435, moved the Duchy of Burgundy from a position of alliance with England to alignment with France, freeing French resources to use against England and also terminating Burgundian support for the English claim to the throne of France. Matters were made worse in 1443 by an expensive and ill-fated campaign in Gascony. The Gascon campaign was commanded by John Beaufort, who had just been elevated from Earl of Somerset to Duke, and was a disaster. Forces that Richard of York needed to hold Normandy were squandered in Gascony, achieving nothing. Beaufort died, possibly by suicide, in 1444.

Richard's disaffection with the situation in England, and his antipathy for the Beaufort family, may have stemmed from this incident. His own position was diminished by the appointment of Beaufort to command the Gascon campaign; effectively Richard went from Royal Lieutenant in France to merely being responsible for Normandy. Richard returned to England in 1445, where he opposed the recent peace agreement with France. Quite possibly as a move to get him away from court, Richard was appointed Lieutenant of Ireland in 1448. The Lieutenancy of France passed to another member of the Beaufort family: Edmund, Earl of Somerset. Edmund was elevated to Duke of Somerset in 1448, as his older brother John had been, but he was equally unsuccessful in France.

Ireland was an important posting, but not as prestigious as France. An appointment intended to last for ten years would keep him out of court politics for that time, whilst retaining the polite fiction that the lieutenancy was an honour and a necessity. However, Richard of York did not reach Ireland until 1449, having been busy with the management

THE HOUSE OF LANCASTER

THE HOUSE OF Lancaster took its name from the Duchy of Lancaster, which had its origins in the Second Barons' War of 1264–7. After the defeat of the barons, Henry III stripped lands from the leaders of the revolt, notably Simon de Montfort, Earl of Leicester, and gave them to his second son, Edmund. These holdings became the Earldom of Lancaster.

The first Duke of Lancaster was Henry of Grosmount, who was elevated from earl largely for his exceptional service in the wars against France. The title then passed to John of Gaunt, who was married to Henry's daughter. John of Gaunt was the son of Edward III, and was extremely powerful while his nephew Richard II was too young to rule in his own right.

John of Gaunt died in 1399, and his lands were seized by Richard II. John's son and heir, Henry Bolingbroke, then returned from exile and deposed Richard, becoming the first English king of the house of Lancaster. His son Henry V and grandson Henry VI continued Lancastrian rule until Henry was deposed in 1461. From 1422 to 1453, Henry was also King of France, although this was disputed.

Henry was briefly reinstalled as king of England from 1470–1, after which he died in captivity in the Tower of London. His only son, Edward, was killed in battle in 1471, after which Henry Tudor became the main royal candidate for the Lancastrian cause. However, his reign as Henry VII was the beginning of a new Tudor dynasty rather than a continuation of Lancastrian rule.

Left: Lancaster was a holding of Simon de Montfort, who met his death in battle against Prince Edward (Edward III) leading the forces of his father, King Henry III. It passed into the possession of the royal family and eventually became a duchy.

THE HOUSE OF YORK

LIKE THE HOUSE of Lancaster, the House of York was descended from the English Plantagenet dynasty. The first Duke of York was Edmund of Langley, fourth son of Edward III, who served as regent while Richard II was on campaign and held other important posts. His elevation to Duke of York came in 1385.

Edmund of Langley moved to oppose the landing by Henry Bolingbroke (Henry IV) in 1399 but instead decided to support him in deposing Richard II. However, the House of York was soon at odds with the ruling Lancastrian dynasty. Edmund's son Edward of Norwich (the second Duke of York) was killed in battle at Agincourt, whilst in the same year his second son, Richard of Conisburgh, was implicated in the Southampton Plot against Henry V and was beheaded.

Richard of Conisburgh was the father of Richard Plantagenet, Duke of York, who was the main Yorkist candidate for the throne and leader of the York faction until his death in 1460. Conisburgh's grandson became Richard III and was the last Plantagenet king of England; his only legitimate son, Edward of Middleham, died in 1484.

Richard III's niece, Elizabeth of York, married Henry Tudor – the best remaining Lancastrian candidate for the throne – and together they began the Tudor dynasty that included Henry VIII and Elizabeth I. Their emblem was the red and white Tudor Rose, symbolizing the joining of the two great houses and the end of a very bloody period in English history.

Right: Edmund of Langley was the first Duke of York. He was brother to Edward, the Black Prince, and John of Gaunt. He campaigned in France on several occasions, fighting alongside the Black Prince at the siege of Limoges.

Above: Humphrey Duke of Gloucester was a strong proponent of war with France, and was an enemy of the Beaufort family from 1425 onwards. Initially restrained by his friend the Duke of Bedford, Gloucester's enmity became ever deeper after Bedford's death.

of his estates and other pressing matters until then. He continued to be a harsh critic of policies towards France, urging war rather than the current attempts at creating a lasting peace, but was unable to wield much influence at such a great distance.

Conflicts over the Regency

At the time Henry V died in 1422, Henry VI was less than a year old. His grandfather on his mother's side, Charles VI of France, died two months later making the baby Henry technically also King of France. He was not crowned until 1429 in England and the following year in France, but even after this he was still a child and did not wield power.

In the interim, Henry's realm was administered by a council of great nobles headed by his uncle, Humphrey, Duke of Gloucester. Humphrey was the youngest of Henry V's brothers, and apparently quite

---

'Henry VI was not crowned until 1429 in England and the following year in France, but even after this he was still a child and did not wield power'.

---

loyal to him. When Gloucester was wounded at Agincourt his brother the king personally defended him against French knights. Humphrey had headed the enquiry into the Southampton Plot and was a logical choice for the role of Lord Protector while Henry V's son and successor was a baby, although his claim was contested by others.

The role of Lord Protector was to be carried out by Gloucester and his older brother, John of Lancaster, Duke of Bedford. However, as Regent of France, Bedford was fully occupied with wars against the French. Although repeatedly asked by opponents of Gloucester to come home and take up the regency in England, Bedford did not do so. Instead he defeated the French, despite the intercession of Joan of Arc, making possible the coronation of Henry VI as King of France.

Among Gloucester's chief opponents was Cardinal Henry Beaufort, who had more than once held the post of Lord Chancellor of England. Cardinal Beaufort presided over the trial of Joan of Arc and condemned her to death in 1431, after which he gradually withdrew from prominence. John of Bedford died in

Above: Cardinal Henry Beaufort was the son of John of Gaunt, and a long-term opponent of Gloucester. He was a proponent of peace with France, eventually managing to bring about a truce in 1444.

1435, leaving Humphrey of Gloucester as heir presumptive and regent. For a time he was extremely powerful but his influence over the court was diminished and eventually eclipsed by William, Earl of Suffolk, who was a favourite of the young king and used this patronage for his own advancement.

Suffolk was an earl until 1444, when a combination of an alliance with Cardinal Beaufort and his negotiation of the Treaty of Tours earned him elevation to marquess. The treaty included an agreement to cede Maine and Anjou to the French crown in return for a marriage between Henry VI and Margaret of Anjou. The fact that land was being given away was concealed from Parliament.

> 'Although the regency had ended when Henry came of age, the struggle to control power over his realm went on around him unabated'.

Gloucester was popular with the people of London and other areas where he held office, but was marginalized at court and eventually brought down by his enemies. His second wife, Eleanor Cobham, was accused of witchcraft against the king. Her associates were charged with necromancy and sentenced to death; she was forced to divorce Humphrey of Gloucester and imprisoned. This brought disgrace upon Gloucester, who was eventually arrested for treason in 1447. He died within days, although probably of natural causes rather than – as rumours at the time suggested – poisoning.

Gloucester's arrest was at the instigation of Suffolk, who continued to enjoy royal favour. However, by 1446, the agreement to give up Maine and Anjou had become public knowledge, arousing great displeasure and fierce opposition from nobles such as Richard of York. This was one reason for sending York to Ireland. Suffolk was elevated to Duke of Somerset in 1448 and given several prestigious roles including Lord High Admiral of England. He dominated the court at this time, with Henry VI almost entirely under his influence. However, a series of disasters in France resulted in the loss of large amounts of territory and compounded ill-feeling over his having negotiated the Treaty of Tours.

Increasing unpopularity and his responsibility for the numerous setbacks in France brought Suffolk under suspicion and in 1450 he was arrested. Henry VI intervened on his friend's behalf but was unable to prevent him being sentenced to a five-year period of exile. Suffolk embarked for Calais but never arrived. On the orders of the Duke of Exeter his vessel was intercepted. He was captured and beheaded.

In the meantime, another royal favourite, Edmund Beaufort, had also been elevated from earl to Duke of Somerset. He attempted to reverse the recent losses in France but was unsuccessful. By 1453, the only French territory remaining in English hands was Calais. Henry VI was at this time in his early thirties, and should have been quite capable of managing the affairs of state. However, he was a weak and easily-led individual whose court was dominated by favourites like Somerset. Although the regency had ended when Henry came of age, the struggle to control power over his realm went on around him unabated.

Opposite: Eleanor Cobham, second wife of Humphrey of Gloucester, was forced to do penance after being accused of necromancy and treason. Her alleged co-conspirators were executed. The affair damaged Gloucester's reputation even though he was not implicated in it.

HACHETTE ET Cⁱᵉ

Sacre de Henri VI á Paris

THE EARLY REIGN OF KING HENRY VI

Henry VI was born on 6 December 1421. His mother, Catherine of Valois, was the daughter of the French King Charles VI. Her marriage to Henry V of England was part of a treaty that had involved long negotiations aimed at settling territorial disputes between England and France.

'He lacked the stubborness required to be a strong king'.

This was less than a complete success; in 1421 Henry V of England once again went on campaign in France. He died there of disease, probably dysentery contracted during his siege of Meaux. This left his infant son as King of England and, when Charles of France died two months later, also of France.

Henry VI was placed in the care of Richard

As a young child, Henry VI was crowned King of England in 1429 and of France in 1431. The marriage of Catherine of Valois (above) and Henry V of England introduced hereditary madness into the English ruling dynasty with dire consequences.

de Beauchamp, Earl of Warwick. Warwick was a loyal supporter of the crown, who had won honours in battle against the rebel Percy family and Owen Glendower, last claimant to be prince of an independent Wales, as well as in France. He was a well-travelled man who had been to the Holy Land as well as Italy, Lithuania, Russia and various German states. In 1428, Warwick was placed in charge of the young king's education, and saw to it that Henry was raised to be a good and pious man. Warwick might have succeeded a little too well in this regard; Henry was a good man, and well educated, but he was no warrior and lacked the stubbornness required to be a strong king. Easily led by those who won his favour, he subsequently allowed his court to be dominated by strong-willed and

CATHERINE OF VALOIS

DAUGHTER OF CHARLES VI of France and Isabella of Bavaria, Catherine was relatively uneducated but was still a desirable marriage prospect for Henry, Prince of Wales (later Henry V). Early proposals came to nothing, not least because the English also wanted land and a large dowry, but eventually an agreement was reached and the Treaty of Troyes was signed in 1420. This came about largely due to the intercession of Catherine's mother, Isabella, who acted as regent while her husband suffered from his frequent bouts of insanity.

Left: Catherine of Valois was not only mother to Henry VI of England, but by her second husband, Owen Tudor, she was grandmother to Henry Tudor whose reign brought the Wars of the Roses to an end.

The Treaty of Troyes did not end conflict between England and France; Catherine's husband Henry V died on campaign in France during 1422. Catherine subsequently married Owen Tudor despite efforts to prevent this by the English great nobility. The eldest of their four children was Edmund of Hadham, Earl of Richmond, whose son was Henry Tudor (Henry VII).

powerful men whose interests were not always aligned with those of England as a nation.

From 1423, the child Henry VI had appeared in public as king, and attended Parliament. His coronation at Westminster was in 1429 and in Paris in 1431. This early period of Henry's reign was characterized by clashes at court between a faction urging greater efforts in the war with France and the pro-peace faction led by the Beaufort family. The pro-war party was headed by Humphrey of Gloucester, who was the most prominent of Henry VI's advisors until Henry came of age in 1442.

After the eclipse of Gloucester, William Duke of Suffolk replaced him as chief advisor. Suffolk urged peace with France and went to considerable lengths to facilitate it. Henry's marriage to Margaret of Anjou was part of this peace process, largely negotiated by Suffolk, and upon her arrival in England he was one of the few people with whom the new queen consort was already acquainted. Suffolk stood as proxy for Henry VI at a wedding ceremony held in France, after which Margaret travelled to England and was married to Henry at Titchfield Abbey in 1445. She was at the time 15 years old, but already displayed the strong personality

Opposite: The coronation of Henry VI was a solemn and grand affair, even though the little boy was incapable of wielding power. In time he would grow into a man scarcely more capable of fulfilling the role of king.

and unwillingness to compromise that would characterize her later role in the Wars of the Roses. Not surprisingly perhaps, she sided with Suffolk and his pro-peace party in court politics.

For his part Suffolk benefited from his friendship with Margaret of Anjou as much as he did from his relationship with the king. His dominance over the English court became almost complete, despite the fact that Margaret was vastly more strong-willed than her husband.

Margaret was not above seeking financial advantages for herself and her favourites, which caused further disaffection among those that lost out as a result.

By 1450, Suffolk had made himself sufficiently unpopular that he was arrested and impeached by Parliament. This permitted Margaret of Anjou to emerge as a force in English politics. Her influence was increased by the birth of a son, Edward, in 1453, but this

Left: Warkworth Castle was the primary holding of Henry Percy, first Earl of Northumberland. The Percy family were important to the security of northern England but became sufficiently powerful that their disputes affected the politics of the whole realm.

Discord in England

In a country ruled by a weak king, disputes between powerful nobles could grow into open warfare. So it was with the feud between the Percy and Neville families. The Percy family were Earls of Northumberland, and had a history of rebellions against the crown. However, after the death of Henry IV there was some reconciliation, and the Percys were primarily charged with protecting the north of England against Scottish incursions.

The Nevilles also held lands in northern England, and it had suited previous monarchs to use them as a counterbalance to the powerful Percy family. Traditionally, the offices of Warden of the East March (centred upon Berwick) and Warden of the West March (centred upon Carlisle) had both been held by the Percy family, but after the rebellions of the early 1400s these offices were transferred to the Nevilles.

year also saw Henry VI suffer the first of several bouts of madness. This created the need for a Lord Protector to govern while Henry was incapacitated, in turn bringing about decades of power struggles.

Right: Margaret of Anjou was almost a complete opposite of her husband; a strong-willed and arrogant woman who did not mind offending everyone around her. She did share a love of scholarship with Henry VI, but in few other ways were they alike.

Although the Percy family was given back the East March in 1417, the office of Warden of the West March remained in Neville hands. These appointments carried with them a great deal of power and prestige, and frequent skirmishing with Scotland gave the Wardens a body of experienced troops. They were also financially valuable, with funds provided by the crown to the Wardens. This was the subject of some contention, as the crown failed to pay what was owed at times, but overall the office of Warden was a powerful and valuable position to hold.

Relations between the Neville and Percy families were not improved by the fact that they had fought on opposite sides in the rebellions

---

'Although the Percy family was given back the East March in 1417, the office of Warden of the West March remained in Neville hands'.

---

of the early 1400s, and as the Nevilles recruited men from the local area to serve under the Warden of the West Marches, further contention resulted. Many of these men owed allegiance to the Percy family, who owned the lands that they lived upon. This overlapping of family lands with royal appointments was made worse by the fact that the Nevilles were in a better financial position and could support the local region better than its Percy lords.

Whilst campaigning against Scotland, forces loyal to the Percys marched through part of the West March without requesting

permission. This was something of a diplomatic incident, which could have been resolved by a strong king. Henry VI was anything but that, and in the absence of royal intervention relations between the Neville and Percy families gradually escalated into open conflict. The

Right: Raby castle was built in the late 1330s by John Neville. Feuding between the Neville and Percy families predated the Wars of the Roses, and carried on as part of the larger conflict.

appointment of William Percy as Bishop of Carlisle was taken as an affront by the Nevilles, and soon both families were waging a low-level campaign of harassment against one another. Skirmishes were fought, but much of the early conflict took the form of destroyed property and intimidation of people loyal to the opposing family. Henry VI issued repeated demands for the conflict to cease, but these were simply ignored by all involved.

The first serious blow was struck by Thomas, Lord Egremont, of the Percy family against

Richard Neville, Earl of Salisbury. The intent was to prevent a wedding that would cause what had previously been Percy lands from passing into Neville control. Neville's escort was allegedly attacked near York but was able to fight its way to safety. There is, however some controversy surrounding this event. A skirmish is recorded as having taken place, but there is no evidence of any casualties on either side. Whatever the truth may be, the conflict now escalated into open raiding of one another's lands, which was prevented from becoming an all-out civil war by the threat of action against both sides by the crown. This was finally taken seriously enough to cause some cooling off in the dispute, although there were armed clashes late in 1454. The Nevilles aligned themselves with Richard, Duke of York, to great mutual benefit. Initially this facilitated the installation of Richard as Lord Protector; in the long run it placed the Nevilles and the Percys on opposite sides in the Wars of the Roses.

Whilst the Percys and the Nevilles were feuding in the north of England, the West Country was also the scene of conflict between noble houses. The Bonville family, headed

Right: Sir Henry Percy, better known as Harry Hotspur, made a name for himself fighting against the Scots. His increasing disaffection with the reign of Henry IV, arising in part from debts owed by the crown, led to him rebelling against the crown.

by William, Lord Bonville, began to grow in power during the 1430s. This created concern among the rival Courtenay family, who held the earldom of Devon. In 1437, William Bonville was granted stewardship of the Duchy of Cornwall, a royal possession. Stewardship would be extremely lucrative and would also advance the prestige of the Bonvilles. The following year the Earl of Devon requested stewardship of the Duchy, which was granted by Henry VI despite the previous appointment.

Although attempts were made to reverse the king's decision, conflict broke out between Bonville and Courtenay supporters, which went on until 1444 when Bonville was appointed to the post of Seneschal of Gascony. Upon his return in 1447, he was granted additional titles and increased in power, aligning himself with the Lancastrian faction at court. This pushed the Courtenay family into the Yorkist camp.

However, alliance between York and the Neville family caused the Courtenays to transfer their allegiance to the Lancastrian faction from 1455 onwards; the Bonvilles switched their loyalty to the Yorkist faction. Violence went on throughout 1455, during which Bonville was supported by York's protectorate. This allowed the Bonvilles to become the dominant force in the West Country, and the feud gradually wound down. The Earl of Devon died in 1458, and as Bonville aged he became less active in the political arena. He met his death in 1461 whilst escorting Henry VI, who was a prisoner of the Yorkist

JACK CADE *in* Cannon Street *declaring himself* LORD *of the* CITY *of* LONDON.

faction at the time of their defeat in the Battle of St Albans. Bonville remained with the king when the Yorkist army fled, having promised to protect him. For this worthy deed he was put to death at the orders of Margaret of Anjou and her young son Edward.

Jack Cade's Rebellion

John Cade, better known as Jack Cade, is credited with leading a major rebellion in Kent in 1450. The leader of the rebels used the identity John Mortimer, identifying with the Earls of March who had a strong claim to the throne. It is not clear whether Jack Cade was the initial leader of the rebels, or whether he assumed this position later, although he was definitely in command when the rebels entered London in early July.

Cade's origins are similarly ambiguous. Cade was probably a commoner who had served in France as a footsoldier. As such, he felt much of the disaffection of the populace with a weak and corrupt monarchy. Loss of

territories in France further weakened support for Henry VI, and rumours had begun to circulate about retribution for the death of the Duke of Suffolk, whose beheaded body was found on the shore at Dover.

Whether or not the threat of retaliation against the commoners of Kent was credible, there were sufficient grievances to cause serious

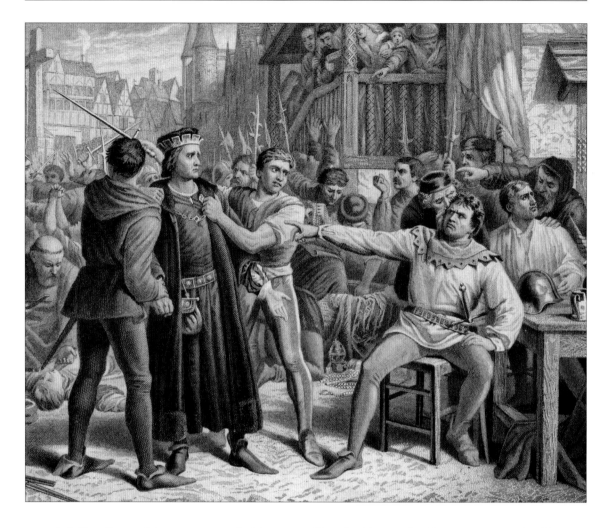

Above: Lord Say was given the merest pretence of a trial by Cade and his followers. Whether or not the case against him was valid, his fate was sealed from the moment he was delivered up to the rebels.

unrest. A list of complaints was created citing corruption, oppression and the failure of the king to censure his favourites for a variety of injustices, and when this achieved nothing an armed uprising began.

With around 5000 ill-equipped but angry commoners, and a scattering of soldiers who had returned from France, gathering near London, the king sent a small force to disperse the rebellion. It was ambushed at Sevenoaks and its leaders killed. The rest of the force was driven off, causing panic among the king's supporters in London. Many in London thought the rebels' demands were acceptable, although Margaret of Anjou was not one of them. The king, for his part, was clearly frightened by the situation. Some of his soldiers and even a few among the nobility had begun to demand that he give the rebels what they wanted. This included the surrender of Lord Say and his son-in-law, William Crowmer.

King Henry ordered these men to be imprisoned in the Tower of London, claiming that he intended to put them on trial for their alleged crimes. Whatever his intentions, this action did nothing to appease his mutinous soldiers who began to pillage the city. Unable to rely upon his own forces, the king fled to Warwickshire and took refuge in Kenilworth castle.

The rebels entered London on 3 July 1450, while the populace vacillated about whether or not to oppose them. At first Cade managed to maintain some discipline among his followers, but soon there was widespread looting that was made worse by further arrivals in the city. Hoping to forestall a storming of the Tower of London, its commander surrendered Lord Say and William Crowmer. Lord Say, former Lord High Treasurer, was hated by the rebels for the numerous injustices that were laid at his door. After a mock trial he was beheaded; his son-in-law Crowmer did not even receive a trial. After this the rebels withdrew across London Bridge. They had achieved some successes but quickly the population of the city turned against them.

'Other regions were inspired to revolt, and although little came of these insurrections, they added to the general instability of the country'.

The rebels undermined their own cause by looting and by breaking open London's prisons to swell their numbers. A renewed attempt to enter the capital over London Bridge was met by a small force from the Tower of London and a larger number of citizens of London, who fought the rebels to a bloody standstill. After this an end to the rebellion was negotiated, with all involved being issued a royal pardon. However, on 10 July Henry VI annulled the pardons, claiming that they were not lawful since they had not been approved by Parliament.

Cade was captured on the 12th but before he could be tried he died of wounds received as he resisted arrest. His corpse was put on trial and symbolically put to death whilst his followers were hunted down.

Although the rebellion was suppressed it did have some lasting effects. Other regions were inspired to revolt, and although little came of these insurrections, they added to the general instability of the country and illustrated the weakness of the king. Cade's list of grievances was seen by Richard of York, and upon his return to England he included some of them in his list of reforms. More importantly perhaps, the flight of the king from his own capital – in the face of a mob of commoners rather than an organized military force led by great nobles – showed just how weak the royal position was.

Cade's identity continues to be a mystery. He styled himself 'Captain of Kent', which could have been an affectation or might indicate some experience as a commander. His rebellion, composed largely of ordinary folk, managed to defeat a small but organized military force sent against it, and is recorded as having camped in an orderly manner. It also moved surprisingly quickly for what was surely little more than an armed mob. It is thus possible that Cade had commanded troops before.

The Art of War in the Late Middle Ages

The armies of the Middle Ages were not especially large. English forces sent to the continent often numbered 6000–8000 men, most of whom were archers. Although the noble class still mostly fought on horseback, a shift from cavalry to infantry as the main striking arm had been ongoing for some time. The French clung to the ideal of the knightly charge longer than the English, who were generally more pragmatic about dismounting their men-at-arms than the French, but even they learned the value of armoured infantry.

Right: The Battle of Poitiers in 1356 was a major victory for the English, resulting in the capture of King John of France. This in turn threw France into turmoil, not least due to increased taxation levied to pay the king's ransom.

The backbone of the English armies of the era was the longbowman, whose weapon could shoot 250m (820ft) or more with enough force to penetrate even heavy armour at least some of the time. Hitting a moving man in the head at 50m (164ft) was nothing special to these archers, meaning that even a knight with his visor down risked an arrow through the eyeslit of his helm. While the odds of a penetrating hit were not

> 'The backbone of the English armies of the era was the longbowman, whose weapon could shoot 250m (820ft) or more with enough force to penetrate even heavy armour'.

great, massed archers could shoot fast enough that the law of averages was in their favour no matter how well protected the target might be.

Thus even the most heavily armoured knights risked being wounded or having their horse shot out from under them by an arrow storm long before they could close to use their lance or sword. If they did manage to close with the unarmoured longbowmen the tables were turned, but medieval commanders understood this very well.

Longbowmen were thus protected by infantry including dismounted men-at-arms and commoners armed with weapons such as the billhook. This was a military variant of a common agricultural tool, consisting of a hooked metal blade and a wooden haft. The

Above: Early cannon were virtually useless in open battle, although they made a noise that might frighten the enemy. In siege warfare they were far more effective, enabling walls to be battered down far more efficiently than using earlier machines such as rams and catapults.

bill gave a footsoldier the reach to engage a horseman, who could be cut or hooked and dragged from his mount. Its length also provided a measure of defence against mounted or infantry opponents.

Dismounted men-at-arms were not especially mobile, but were very tough defensively. Their armour was heavy enough that a downed man might struggle to get back up, especially when footing was bad such as on muddy ground, but they were not so encumbered that they could not fight effectively. Many were armed with heavy weapons such as the pollaxe, which had an axe blade backed by a hammer or pick, and a spearpoint for thrusting attacks. Used in both hands, it offered an excellent combination of offensive and defensive capability, allowing the man at arms to successfully engage armoured or unarmoured opponents.

Offensively, the mounted knight or man-at-arms was an extremely potent force on the battlefield, combining mobility with the staying power of heavy armour. Charges were often made at a fairly slow pace, especially if repeated attacks were made by increasingly tired horses, but even at the trot a knight could deliver a powerful assault. The weapon of choice from horseback was the lance, but hand weapons such as axes and maces were highly effective after close combat had been joined.

The sword was a sidearm rather than the main striking tool of the man-at-arms. Its design

THE ARMING SWORD

THE SINGLE-HANDED SWORD used as a sidearm by knights and men-at-arms was known as an arming sword, or sometimes – confusingly – as a short sword. It was not particularly short, except compared to the longsword, which was a two-handed weapon.

Arming sword designs fell into two main types. Some were relatively heavy, relying on impact to penetrate armour, where others were designed to thrust into weak points in an opponent's armour. Neither was totally effective against the heavy plate armour of the 1450s but a skilled swordsman could disable or kill a heavily-protected opponent.

Contrary to popular myth, these swords were not very heavy and were anything but clumsy. Far from swinging massive blows at one another and hoping for the best, medieval swordsmen were well trained and highly skilled.

As such they needed a weapon that balanced precision against impact, and had a good cutting edge. A sword that was too weighty could not move fast enough to strike precisely against a moving opponent, and would not be controllable once it began to swing. It might hit very hard but would only do so by accident.

Thus the arming swords of the late Middle Ages, although visually simple in form, were extremely well made and finely balanced precision tools. The sword was both a symbol of office and a means of staying alive on the battlefield, and as such it was one of the most important items a nobleman could own.

Below: The sword is very much the symbol of nobility, so it is with swords that the foreground figures are armed. An initial charge would far more likely be made with the lance, resorting to the sword as a backup weapon.

Opposite: At the battle of Castillon, the English charge was broken by artillery emplaced in field fortifications, after which a French counterattack ensured that this, the last major action of the Hundred Years War, was a resounding French victory.

had evolved to deal with increasingly heavy armour, but compared to a mace or axe its anti-armour performance was relatively weak. Nevertheless, the sword was the symbol of nobility and a useful backup weapon. Against lightly-armoured opponents it was very effective.

Firearms were making an appearance at this time, although they were extremely primitive and not very effective. 'Hand-gonnes' took the form of a short tube mounted on a stick and fired using a hot coal or a piece of slow-match. Often the hand-gonne was operated by a two-man team, one aiming the weapon (in a very general way) and the other applying the means of ignition. This was hardly conducive to accuracy, but the projectiles from these weapons were not particularly precise in any case. Far more effective were cannon, which had made their noisy but not very influential presence known on battlefields since Crécy. By the closing stages of the Hundred Years War, cannon were reliable enough to be the primary means of bringing down castle defences, and were at least somewhat effective in open battle. The Battle of Castillion, fought in 1543 as the last action of the Hundred Years War, saw the French field an artillery park that may have included as many as 300 various guns. These clumsy early field pieces could not manoeuvre during a battle and were little use except on the defensive, but at Castillion the English force advanced directly at the guns and was shot to pieces in a manner reminiscent of Crécy or Agincourt. Even so, it was a charge by armoured cavalry that broke the English army.

While missile weapons in the form of the longbow and artillery both had a major part to play in weakening an enemy force, the armoured

horseman remained the arm of decision. This would change within a few decades, but the Wars of the Roses were very much a medieval war fought in the traditional manner.

Ransom Demands

One tradition associated with this kind of warfare was that of ransom for a defeated nobleman. Common soldiers might well be put to death if captured, but a knight or higher noble stood a very good chance of being ransomed. Not only did this bring in revenue for those who took the surrender of a lord, but it also helped reduce the damage caused

'The financial cost of ransoming back noblemen captured by their enemies was enormous. Each level of nobility had a ransom associated with their rank'.

by a battlefield disaster. The financial cost of ransoming back noblemen captured by their enemies was enormous. Each level of nobility had a ransom associated with their rank; the term 'king's ransom' was fairly specific in the Middle Ages. Ransom might be paid by the captured knight's lord or king, or he might have to find it himself. Either way, the practice of ransom was a form of life insurance for the nobility. From the point of view of the king and the realm, ransom also helped reduce the disruption caused by a war. The military class were also administrators, many of whom held important offices and all of whom had estates that generated revenue. A death in battle meant an inheritance, which might put an inexperienced lord in charge of a great estate or cause a dispute over who was to receive it. A senior official who was killed had to be replaced, which might disrupt the running of the kingdom or even change the internal balance of power.

A nobleman who was in serious trouble on the battlefield could usually save his own life by surrendering, although he would be well advised to surrender to someone with a title. Commoners might kill him anyway, especially if they thought there was little chance of benefiting from any ransom paid for their captive. Surrendering to a knight of lower status might be a social embarrassment but was probably survivable.

The ransom system could be manipulated in various ways. A great lord or king might

> 'The Wars of the Roses saw several incidents where a notable lord was denied mercy or surrender despite asking for it'.

choose to pay ransoms for his favourites and not for the vassals of his opponents, which would drain them financially. An outstanding ransom could be used as a political bargaining tool. Such was the case with King John II of France, captured by the English in 1356 at the Battle of Poitiers. King John became a prisoner in the Tower of London, although this was more of a house arrest in a royal residence than grim incarceration. He was treated as an honoured guest and rendered the respect due to a monarch, but he was not free until the ransom was paid. France needed money to rebuild the military forces that had taken heavy losses and to pay John's ransom, but struggled to raise either. The ransom demanded by England was impossible to meet, making the treaty that

agreed it invalid. War was renewed, adding to the problems of a France ruled by regency. This led to a second treaty agreeing a lower, but still enormous, ransom and territory to be ceded to England. King John was released in return for other hostages who would be sent to England and remain there until the ransom was finally paid. Among these hostages was Prince Louis, second son of the French king. When the ransom was not paid in the expected time, Louis first tried to negotiate his release and then fled from captivity, returning to France. His father then declared that he must go back into captivity since the hostage sent in his place was no longer in English custody, and voluntarily returned to England as a prisoner. The reasoning behind this has sparked some debate. It may have been a matter of personal honour, or John II may simply have wearied of trying to run a kingdom that was in a shambles. He ended his days as what amounted to an honoured guest in England, living a regal lifestyle without the responsibilities. Although his ransom remained only partly paid, it was still enough to increase English power, whilst France suffered through a period of weak government and internal division.

The Last Resort

Although there were significant financial and political advantages to accepting the surrender of noblemen and ransoming them, the Wars of the Roses saw several incidents where a notable lord was denied mercy or surrender despite asking for it, or where great men were put to death rather than being ransomed. Surrender was always a chancy business, and remained the last resort of the defeated warrior.

Opposite: The surrender of King John and his son at Poitiers was very much a last resort. According to contemporary sources they were virtually alone and surrounded by the English army, but made a spirited stand before being forced to yield.

RICHARD, DUKE OF YORK

The death of Humphrey, Duke of Gloucester, in 1447 made Richard, Duke of York, heir presumptive to the throne of England. He was disaffected with policy towards France, and generally opposed to the circle of favourites at court.

'This collapse was blamed on Henry VI's favourites'.

Richard was also displeased with the treatment he had received while he was Lieutenant of France. All this made Richard a vociferous critic of royal policies, although he was still a servant of the crown and had to be treated with a certain level of respect. The answer was to send him to Ireland on what was on the face of it a prestigious posting as royal representative there. In practice this removed

Richard, Duke of York served the English crown in a variety of important posts, including Lieutenant of France and later of Ireland. He chose not to press his claim to the English throne whilst serving as regent to the insane King Henry VI. (Above) the court of King Henry VI.

him from court politics and allowed Henry VI's favourites to exert their influence unhindered.

In 1450, Richard decided to return from Ireland in response to a series of crises. The rebellion led by Jack Cade had been put down but there was serious unrest elsewhere. Popular demands for the reversal of some of Henry VI's more questionable decisions (notably the grant of titles and lands to his favourites) and the redress of a number of injustices were still circulating, whilst the southeast of England was becoming increasingly lawless. This stemmed largely from the loss of English holdings in Normandy. Townsmen, farmers and soldiers were returning to England, often without money and possessions, and doing whatever they had to in order to survive. The string of defeats that led to this collapse was blamed on Henry VI's favourites and added to the general discontent with the state of the monarchy.

Calls had been made for York to return to England and set things right, although to what extent this was simply wishful thinking on the part of the discontented citizenry is unclear. It is likely that as a vocal opponent of the existing circle of favourites he was seized upon as a source of hope by rebels such as Cade's follower whether or not he had any real sympathy for them. It is unlikely that York came back to England to support the rebels or because they asked him to. More probably his own agenda happened to coincide with that of the king's other opponents, or perhaps he felt that the unstable conditions prevailing in England at the time created a good opportunity for decisive action.

> 'Richard of York landed in Wales in early September 1450 and marched on London. His force was met by a royal army, creating a tense standoff'.

In any case, Richard of York landed in Wales in early September 1450 and marched on London. His force was met by a royal army, creating a tense standoff. Richard at that time did not want conflict, and repeatedly proclaimed that his only intention was to restore good government and oust the circle of favourites surrounding the king. York and Henry VI reached an accommodation, avoiding civil war, and matters stabilized for a time. However, York had failed to obtain any meaningful changes in government. Although the Duke of Somerset

Left: Trim castle in Meath, Ireland, was Richard of York's capital when he served as Lieutenant of Ireland. Its facilities included a royal mint and guest accommodation where dignitaries such as the young Henry V and Humphrey of Gloucester had stayed.

RICHARD, DUKE OF YORK

RICHARD OF YORK was related to Edward III through both his paternal and maternal lines. He was for many years the most powerful nobleman in England, after the king, and held important offices as Lieutenant of France and Lieutenant of Ireland. During the incapacity of Henry VI, Richard of York held the office of Lord Protector, assuming the duties of head of state in place of the insane king.

Although Richard's father, the Earl of Cambridge, was executed for treason against the king, Richard was permitted to inherit

Above: Disputes between noblemen could be resolved by a challenge to single combat, signified by throwing down an armoured gauntlet. Acceptance of the challenge was signified by picking it up, after which details of how and where the duel was to take place were resolved.

much of his property once he came of age. He also gained the estates and titles of the powerful Mortimer family and married into the Nevilles. Richard of York was thus not only powerful but well-connected, and was a natural choice of leader for those who objected to the corruption and favouritism of the court. His importance was such that even though he was an opponent of Henry VI's favourites at court, he was still appointed as Lord Protector.

It is notable that during Richard's first appointment as Lord Protector, his rule was deliberately and scrupulously fair. He advanced his allies, but did not act against his enemies even though he had the power to do so. He recognized Edward, son of Henry VI, as Prince of Wales despite rumours about the boy's parentage, even though this meant that his own claim to the throne as heir presumptive was thus ended.

Nor did he seek to continue the wars with France. The French did not move against Calais and were not, apparently, preparing for an invasion of England, so Richard left the situation in France as he had inherited it. He worked to restore order to the realm as he had always stated was his aim, succeeding in reining in the Percy-Neville feud in the north, but did not attempt to take the throne at this time.

Richard at first attempted to work 'within the system' to bring reform to England, but eventually took up arms against the throne. Had events turned out differently he would have inherited the crown from Henry VI upon his death, but Richard never became king. His sons Edward IV and Richard III did ascend the throne, however.

Right: Richard of York's actions lend credence to his claim that all he wanted was fair governance for England. He did not persecute his enemies whilst Regent, nor did he attempt to take the crown despite having a good opportunity.

was temporarily imprisoned in the Tower of London (possibly for his own protection; he was hated in the increasingly unstable and violent London), York was unable to force Henry VI to prosecute Somerset for his failures in Normandy. Indeed, in 1451 Somerset was appointed Captain of Calais, commander of the last English holding in northern France. Although this took him away from the king, and lessened his ability to influence royal decisions, it was hardly what York had wanted. However, with little support available he could not press hard for reforms.

> 'A son would displace Richard of York from his position as heir presumptive, weakening his position considerably at a time when he was already in eclipse'.

Nevertheless York continued to work against Somerset and to try to build himself a more widespread powerbase. In 1452 he again marched on London, still protesting his loyalty, and presented allegations against Somerset. He also demanded that he be recognized as Henry VI's heir. His claim to this position was solid, but Henry and his supporters favoured someone less directly opposed to their policies. Although an accommodation was again reached between York and Henry VI, York was required to swear not to take up arms against the crown and spent the next few months under arrest.

Right: King Henry VI is depicted here as a listless invalid whilst his favourite Somerset dominates court affairs. Richard of York (left) took extreme measures, including the use of armed force, for lack of any viable alternatives.

Opposite: By placing his hand upon the throne, Richard of York laid claim to it. The resulting Act of Accord, in 1460, agreed that Henry VI would remain king until his death and that the crown would then pass to Richard.

Richard as Lord Protector

In 1453, Margaret of Anjou finally became pregnant. A son would displace Richard of York from his position as heir presumptive, weakening his position considerably at a time when he was already in eclipse. York was lacking much in the way of political backing. His office as Lieutenant of Ireland was taken away, along with the additional office he had been granted during negotiations with Henry, Justice of the Forest South of the Trent.

King Henry was making a point of weakening York's position further by finding against his supporters in any disputes brought before him, and might have continued to do so had he not suddenly been stricken with madness in 1453. Insanity ran in his family but until this point, at the age of 32, he had not exhibited the symptoms shown by 'Charles the Mad' of France or others among Henry's ancestors. The trigger was probably news of the Battle of Castillion, at which an English army was routed after attempting to advance in the face of emplaced cannon. Castillion brought the Hundred Years War with France to an end, with English defeat total and permanent. Henry lapsed into a more or less catatonic state, unresponsive and totally incapable of governing his realm.

Right: Before his insanity manifested itself, 'Charles the Mad' of France was a good and wise ruler whose policies brought about a period of prosperity. His descent into insanity plunged the realm into a power struggle among his council of regents.

At first it was possible to conduct business as usual and hope for a swift recovery, but as Henry's madness continued it became obvious that a Lord Protector had to be appointed. Although Margaret of Anjou and Henry VI's circle of favourites had hoped to be able to control the kingdom, Richard of York was appointed as regent. During the next few months York was unable to undo much of the influence of Henry's favourites, and was kept busy dealing with the troubles of a turbulent realm. With the Nevilles and the Percys in open conflict in the north of the kingdom, York also had to deal with the rebellion of Henry Holland, Duke of Exeter, in 1454. Holland had been Constable of the Tower of London at one point, and was a temperamental and vindictive man. He later became a prominent Lancastrian commander.

Richard of York did have time to preside over Parliament in the king's stead, and in February 1454 Parliament impeached Somerset, although the Lancastrian faction also secured the impeachment of the Yorkist lords Thomas Courtenay, Earl of Devon, and Edward Brooke, Lord Cobham. This stemmed from their part in Richard of York's previous armed standoffs with the crown. Parliament also recognized the king's new son, Edward, as Prince of Wales, but was unable to resolve a number of financial problems. York installed several of his allies in key positions but was not able to bring Somerset to trial. He did, however, keep him imprisoned and took from him the office of Captain of Calais. This York transferred to himself, although he did not keep it long.

Recovery from Madness

At the end of 1454, Henry VI recovered from his madness, and by February 1455 he was able to take up his duties once more, although he seemed to suffer from memory problems. Notably, he did not appear to have any knowledge of his son, Edward. His enemies had been claiming that Edward was fathered not by Henry but by Somerset, although this was probably nothing more than a smear campaign. Nevertheless, Henry's lack of recognition of the child fuelled these rumours.

Richard of York was no longer needed as Lord Protector and was dismissed, whilst his enemy the Duke of Somerset was released

Below: The Talbot Shrewsbury Book was presented to Margaret of Anjou to celebrate her betrothal to Henry VI. It contained 15 French texts ranging from fiction to treatises on the conduct of warfare. The book survives to this day.

from imprisonment and returned to favour. York lost the office of Captain of Calais, which returned to Somerset whilst the court became increasingly dominated by Margaret of Anjou, whose position had been strengthened by the birth of her son. Ministers appointed by Richard of York during his tenure as Lord Protector

> 'By February 1455 Henry VI was able to take up his duties once more, though he seemed to suffer from memory problems'.

were dismissed and replaced with men favoured by the king's faction.

These developments worried York and his supporters, and when the king summoned a council to be held at Leicester, they resolved to act. The council was not a Parliament, and did not include any of York's supporters. Its ostensible purpose was to provide security for the king against his enemies, so it was not hard to see where the wind was blowing. York, along with his allies the Earls of Warwick and Salisbury – both named Richard Neville – feared that this council would vote to censure them or at the very least otherwise act against their interests. Arrest and possible execution were entirely possible. Somerset and his faction had pushed hard for action against the Yorkist faction as soon as they were restored to power, even though the Yorkists had been deliberately

Right: Margaret of Anjou was one of the major players in the Wars of the Roses, repeatedly returning from apparent defeat to make a new effort at putting her son on the throne of England. She is commemorated with this statue in Paris.

keeping a low profile and had acted honourably during the protectorate.

There seemed to be no option but armed resistance, although in all probability York hoped for another standoff rather than open combat with the royal army. He marched with his allies to intercept the king, hoping to prevent him from reaching Leicester and the great council. Both forces met at St Albans, north of London.

The First Battle of St Albans

York had with him around 3000 men as he advanced to meet the king's force, with more joining him along the way. He was at Royston on 20 May 1455 when he issued a statement explaining his actions. York maintained that he had been forced into armed confrontation by the summoning of the great council directed

against supposed enemies of the king, and from which he had been deliberately excluded.

On the 21st, at Ware, York wrote to the king himself. His carefully and humbly worded letter proclaimed his loyalty and reverence for the king, but demanded immediate access in order make his Majesty aware of the lies being told about the Yorkists by their enemies, who were by inference also the enemies or at least not good friends of the king. Somerset had at that time around 3000 soldiers under his command, although this force was greatly augmented by the presence of numerous nobles and their

Below: St Albans was unwalled but the Lancastrian army was able to improvize barricades. However, defending the barricades required most of the Lancastrian manpower, enabling Warwick's troops to break through elsewhere.

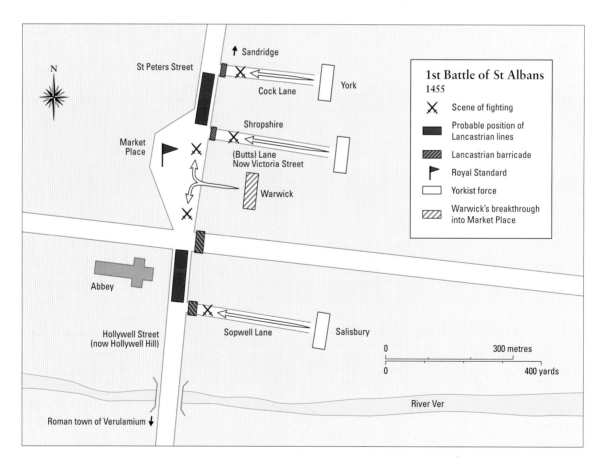

retinues. Additional reinforcements were hurriedly being raised and marched to Leicester, but for the time being Somerset felt vulnerable. He thus took up position in the unwalled town of St Albans, creating barricades to protect his position.

A standoff ensued at St Albans on 22 May. As York's army approached, the king sent Humphrey Stafford, Duke of Buckingham, to meet him. Buckingham demanded an explanation from York for why he was in arms against the king, and York repeated the sentiments he had expressed by letter. He professed loyalty to the king and to the nation, maintaining that all he wanted was to restore good government and remove the circle of self-interested individuals who were leading the king astray. This parlay was conducted in the manner of the time, through messengers and heralds, and was slow going. Richard of York was aware of the vulnerable position of the royal force, and that sooner or later reinforcements would arrive to remedy that weakness. He wanted a response immediately, and

was not prepared to accept vague assurances that the matter would receive attention. He had heard that before, in 1452, and nothing had come of it.

York eventually demanded the arrest of Somerset pending a trial for treason. This, and York's refusal to accept Henry's – probably well-intentioned but vague – assurances of justice, annoyed the king greatly. Normally a rather gently-spoken man, Henry responded to the demands with a violent outburst and a declaration that he would crush those before him. Henry called the Yorkists traitors in this outburst. If there was a single moment when civil war became inevitable, this was it. York, hearing of the king's response from his returning herald, knew that there was no longer any chance of reform from 'within the system'. Worse, the king was now openly in arms against him. The Yorkists likely faced a grim fate if they surrendered or were defeated, so the only remaining option was to fight and win.

York delivered a speech to his troops, in which he told them that since the king had

ON THIS SITE STOOD THE CASTLE INN BEFORE WHICH EDMUND BEAUFORT 2ND DUKE OF SOMERSET, WAS SLAIN DURING THE 1ST BATTLE OF ST ALBANS 22ND MAY 1455.

JOHN AND EDMUND BEAUFORT, DUKES OF SOMERSET

JOHN AND EDMUND Beaufort were descendants of John of Gaunt and thus members of the House of Lancaster. In 1418 or 1419, John Beaufort inherited the Earldom of Somerset from his elder brother Henry; the latter was killed at the Siege of Rouen. John was subsequently captured at the Battle of Baugé in 1421 and held prisoner until ransomed.

Despite an inauspicious career so far, John Beaufort was elevated to Duke of Somerset in 1443 and was also given the Earldom of Kendal. He was sent to Gascony in command of an attempt to retake lands lost there that increased friction with Richard of York, whose authority as Lieutenant of France was undermined by the appointment. Matters were made worse when a large sum of money was given to Beaufort whilst Richard of York was in debt from supporting the English campaign in France out of his own pocket.

John Beaufort's campaign in Gascony was a disaster for himself and for England. Commanding around 7000 men, which was a good-sized force for the period, Beaufort achieved nothing and eventually returned to England in disgrace. He died in 1444, quite likely by suicide, and the position of head of the Beaufort family passed to his younger brother Edmund. Edmund Beaufort was a much more successful commander than this brother, and achieved notable successes at Harfleur and Calais. He was created Earl of Dorset in 1442 and elevated to Marquess in 1443. Edmund had inherited the Earldom of Somerset from his disgraced brother, and in 1448 was elevated to Duke.

Somerset was a favourite of Henry VI. He used this relationship to obtain a number of high offices, which carried with them both power and a large income. Among these was the position of Lieutenant of

Left: John Beaufort was the first Duke of Somerset, but was not successful as a military commander. The title of Duke of Somerset was re-created for his brother Edmund, creating confusion as to whether Edmund was first or second to hold that title.

Right: The battle of Formigny in 1450 was a decisive defeat for the English, whose holdings in France were being rapidly overrun. With the English army broken there was little to prevent the French from retaking the rest of Normandy.

France, to which he was appointed in 1448. The previous holder of this office was Richard of York, whose subsequent posting to Ireland did little to appease his resentment at losing such an important office. Somerset took command in France at a bad time. From 1449, the French made a series of gains that drove the English from almost all of northern France. Within another three years, English holdings in southern France were also lost. It is possible that the failure of the crown to pay Somerset a large amount of money promised when he took up the office of Lieutenant of France was a contributory factor in these disasters. The English presence in France had been propped up for some time from the personal coffers of its commanders, draining the resources of the vastly wealthy Duke of York. Somerset had nothing like the funds available to York, and

lacking Royal money he may simply have not been able to maintain his forces.

Somerset returned to England and was able to dominate the court of the weak Henry VI until the latter lapsed into insanity in 1453. Somerset was imprisoned in the Tower of London during the First Protectorate of Richard of York, but released when York was dismissed from this post upon Henry's recovery in 1454.

Somerset was one of the key players in English politics for the next few months, and was on his way to Leicester with the king when confronted by Yorkist forces at St Albans. Somerset was killed during the collapse of the royal army that followed and his son Henry Beaufort was wounded. The latter survived to become a key Lancastrian commander before changing sides to serve Edward VI for a time.

killed. Panic spread through the royalist army, during which some notables fled – among them the bearer of the royal standard, Sir Philip Wentworth. Several other important men were killed, including Thomas de Clifford and Henry Percy, Earl of Northumberland. The Dukes of Buckingham and Somerset were captured after suffering wounds.

The battle lasted less than an hour all told, and ended with numerous members of the great nobility dead or captured. Among the latter was Henry VI, who did nothing but observe the battle. He was slightly wounded by a stray arrow but otherwise unharmed when the Yorkists reached him. Unusually for such an engagement, the proportion of the 100-odd casualties fell worst upon the nobility. This was

> 'The battle lasted less than an hour all told, and ended with numerous members of the great nobility dead or captured. Among the latter was Henry VI'.

Above: Henry VI is said to have taken little notice during the battle of St Albans. He was taken into a nearby house by his entourage, where Richard of York came to him, simultaneously apologizing and taking the king captive.

refused to listen to his petition and condemned them all as traitors, there was no longer any choice but to fight. Around noon he sent his force in three columns against the barricades surrounding St Albans. These were stoutly held, and the Yorkist assault was driven back from all three approaches. But while the outnumbered royal force was concentrating on defending the barricades, the young Richard Neville, Earl of Warwick, led his personal troops through houses at the southeast side of the town and into the middle of the royal position. This bold move caught the defenders by surprise, although they attempted to repel the new assault. The royal force managed to hold its own for a time, but collapsed after the Duke of Somerset was

partly due to the collapse of the royal army, in which lightly equipped footsoldiers and archers could flee whilst heavily-armoured men fighting on foot were slower to retire.

The massacres and executions that characterized later actions of the Wars of the Roses did not take place at St Albans. John Sutton de Dudley, Lord Dudley, was the only nobleman sent to the Tower of London, and he was freed fairly quickly. Most others were deprived of their arms and armour, which were extremely valuable, but either freed or placed under the relatively benign supervision of Yorkist leaders. Many of those captured at St Albans

ARMOUR PROTECTION

BY THE MID-1400s, armour technology had reached a high level of sophistication. Armour was made from good-quality steel which combined protection with relative lightness, and generally took the form of articulated plates that did not greatly hinder mobility. Chain mail was used to reinforce or cover areas that were hard to protect with plates, but it was a secondary component.

Plate armour provided greater protection than the preceding chain mail for the same weight of metal, and also distributed that weight much better. Armour was shaped to deflect blows as well as acting as a physical barrier to prevent penetration, and thus worked much better when the wearer was able to move, causing attacks to glance off rather than striking full-on.

An armoured man on a horse was an extremely difficult opponent to deal with. Even if surrounded, his horse could often push through the press and permit an escape, whereas a man on foot might not be able to break free. Dragging a knight off his mount was a common infantry tactic, therefore, with some weapons being specially adapted to catch on armour plates and facilitate this.

The idea that armour was so heavy that knights had to be assisted or even winched onto their mounts is a myth; some men could vault onto their horses in full armour. However, armour was still heavy and tiring to wear, and made it difficult to rise if the wearer was downed. No matter how good the protection, there were gaps that could be exploited if the armoured warrior were downed and held immobile.

Thus armour did not make the wearer invulnerable, but it did act as a 'force-multiplier', enabling an armoured man to survive blows that would put an unprotected warrior out of the fight. So long as he could avoid being swarmed, an armoured knight was a match for several 'lesser' soldiers.

Right: Armour was shaped to deflect blows as well as to resist them, making it extremely hard to land a lethal strike on a man-at-arms who could move. There were weak and unprotected areas, but these were not vulnerable whilst the knight remained on his horse.

agreed to accept the new situation, in which Henry was taken to London as a prisoner and York reinstalled as Lord Protector. This was ratified by Parliament in November 1455. Henry may have suffered another bout of insanity during the battle; some accounts mention him being in an oblivious waking stupor when found by the Yorkists.

Margaret of Anjou was tasked with looking after her husband during this period, whilst York ran the country. She maintained that her son Edward, Prince of Wales, must inherit the throne whilst others preferred York as heir. The question remained unresolved in 1456 when Henry regained his senses and resumed his role as king. He remained unpopular in London but he had a good amount of support elsewhere. As a result he moved his court to Coventry and dismissed Richard of York as Lord Protector for a second time.

York was sent to Ireland, resuming his previous post as Royal Lieutenant there, whilst Henry once more surrounded himself with favourites. Among them was Henry Beaufort, Duke of Somerset. The new Duke of Somerset resented York for the role he had played in the death of his father at St Albans and for the wounds he had received in that battle. He was to become a major Lancastrian commander as the Wars of the Roses escalated, but for a time there was relative peace.

Right: Thomas Bourchier, Archbishop of Canterbury, was a descendent of Edward III although very far from the line of succession. His 'Loveday' ceremony was intended to heal the rifts between the great nobility, but in practice achieved nothing of lasting importance.

The Loveday

Attempts to make this peace permanent resulted in a long series of settlements and agreements designed to resolve feuds and settle disputes, culminating in a procession to St Paul's Cathedral and a ceremony to celebrate the new spirit of peace and brotherhood now filling the land. This event, known as the 'Loveday', took place in March 1458 and was led by the Archbishop of Canterbury. Since the Loveday had the support of the Church and the king, the great nobility had to at least pay lip-service to its intentions. However, that was about all it achieved. Within a year open conflict had resumed, and the wars took on an increasingly bitter and vindictive tone. In the first phase of the conflict there were protestations of loyalty to the crown and the courtesies of the feudal system were generally upheld. After 1458, this was not the case. Defeat in battle often meant execution, and with neither side offering quarter there was little incentive to restrain the savagery of war.

THE PARLIAMENT OF DEVILS

Richard Neville, Earl of Warwick, was a close supporter of the Yorkist faction. He gained popularity in and around London by protecting the interests of the merchant class, and campaigning against piracy in the English Channel.

◆

'Ignoring a royal summons would be seen as open defiance'.

Warwick's appointment as Captain of Calais may have been in part to get him away from court, where he had been able to protect prominent Yorkists from the machinations of their opponents. His appointment was logical, however, in that he was an experienced commander. England's last territory in France was an obvious target for attempts to retake it, and required a standing force to defend the port. This required a leader

A possession of the Earl of Warwick, the impressive Warwick Castle was, for a few months in 1469, the prison for Edward IV. Warwick was forced to release the king, but soon began plotting against him once more. Earl of Warwick (Above).

who could be relied upon to keep the force in good fighting condition and to repel any attempt at aggression. Warwick could also use the port as a base to suppress piracy in the Channel.

This was, however, a double-edged sword as it gave Warwick yet another source of income with which to further his plans. It also placed him in command of the only permanent military force in England other than the retinues maintained by the great nobility. Worries over what Warwick might do with his forces prompted the crown to withhold funds and supplies for a time, but the need to protect Calais overrode concerns about its commander's actions. The need for a strong position in Calais was underlined in August 1457 with French attack on Sandwich in Kent. A force of around 4000 men attacked the town and destroyed much of it, raising concerns of an invasion to follow.

This never came, but Warwick began to exert more aggressive control over the Channel in any case. This created tension with the Hanseatic League, a mercantile organization that held territories along the North Sea and Baltic coasts, especially when Warwick's ships captured a fleet carrying salt. Warwick's vessels also attacked ships belonging to the Kingdom of Castile. Far from suppressing piracy in the Channel, Warwick was enriching himself by piratical means, and creating international incidents that might lead to conflicts England could not afford.

Left: Like all great lords, Warwick had his own seal. In theory a sealed document had the authority of the owner of that seal, although in Warwick's mind his authority was somewhat greater than his official status implied.

'Warwick was recalled to court in order to explain himself. He arrived in Westminster but somehow became involved in a skirmish...'

Warwick was recalled to court in order to explain himself. He arrived in Westminster but somehow became involved in a skirmish with members of the royal household. Warwick claimed that this had been a deliberate attempt on his life and fled the capital. It may have been such, or an attempt to quietly arrest him away from the main body of his troops that was resisted, or it may even have been engineered by Warwick and his supporters as an excuse not to face the judgement of the court.

Whatever the case, Warwick returned to his ships and sailed for Calais. He was subsequently summoned, along with York and Salisbury, to a council at Coventry. All three declined to attend, considering the risk of arrest too great. There were solid grounds for such suspicion – a noble surrounded by an army or in a friendly castle would require great effort to arrest if he chose to resist, and this would create an incident of open conflict that might have other repercussions. A quiet arrest when he had only a handful of retainers to protect him, and was on ground controlled by the arresting faction, was simpler and less costly to accomplish. It was also much easier to control news of the circumstances surrounding the arrest if it were not done openly.

Thus the main Yorkists were placed in a position where they had to defy royal authority in order to protect their safety. They no longer felt that they were protected by the social structure they were part of, and could not rely upon the honourable conduct of their enemies. A second phase of the Wars of the Roses was about to begin, one in which the situation changed from internal political machinations to a straight fight between the King of England and his enemies.

The Battle of Blore Heath

Richard of York realized that ignoring a royal summons would be seen as open defiance and perhaps even treason, and began marshalling forces for the conflict that was likely to soon begin. He raised his own army and instructed his supporters to gather at Ludlow Castle in the Welch Marches. Ludlow was a logical choice as it was one of Richard's main strongholds, but it could also have been seen as symbolic in some ways. Ludlow was a holding of the Mortimer family, whose claim to the throne had been a rallying point for rebels in the past – Jack Cade had used the name 'Mortimer' for this reason. Whether or not this was an element in York's choice, or whether it concerned his allies and

Below: Blore Heath favoured the Lancastrian army, which had numbers and position to its advantage as well as the strategic initiative. The Lancastrians just had to block the Yorkist advance.

enemies, the king acted quickly – although unsuccessfully – to prevent a junction of the Yorkist forces.

Richard Neville, Earl of Salisbury, marched from Middleham Castle in Yorkshire towards Ludlow. He had around 5000 men with him, whilst a Lancastrian force of about twice the size waited on the moorland at Blore Heath. The forces met on 23 September 1459. Although the Lancastrians were concealed behind a hedge, their banners were spotted and Salisbury's force halted to deploy. Although he had forestalled an ambush, Salisbury was in a bad position. He was outnumbered two to one, with the Lancastrian force across his path and a wood behind making retreat problematic. A stream running between the two forces made an attack difficult for whichever side took the initiative. The Lancastrian commander, Baron Audley, could probably afford to wait. His mission was

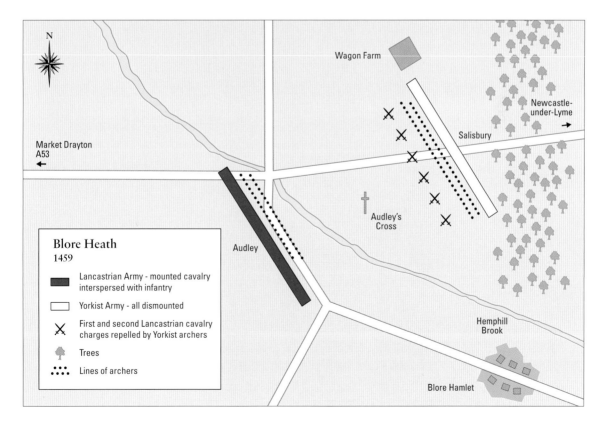

Right: Although not present with the Lancastrian army, legend has it that Margaret of Anjou observed the battle of Blore Heath from a nearby church tower. She fled when it became obvious that the day was lost.

to prevent a junction of Yorkist forces and he was doing so. He could reasonably expect to stand in his defensive position and await the attack that Salisbury would inevitably have to deliver.

As was typical of the era, the battle opened with an exchange of heralds, who carried to words of the commanders back and forth in an extended parlay. When this broke down, archers on both sides began a long-range skirmish that proved equally inconclusive. Salisbury then ordered part of his force to retire as if he

> 'Audley was killed in the fighting, and when a third attack was also repelled, some elements of the Lancastrian forces switched sides'.

planned to break contact. This prompted the Lancastrian force to attack, which under other circumstances might have been a decisive blow. However, as the Lancastrian cavalry struggled to cross the steep-sided stream, Salisbury's men advanced to meet them and drove them back with heavy losses. A second assault succeeded in forcing a crossing, but could not break the Yorkist force. Audley was killed in the fighting, and when a third attack was also repelled, some elements of the Lancastrian forces switched sides. Salisbury took advantage of the confusion to launch his own attack, which routed the Lancastrians. The Lancastrian army reportedly suffered around 2000 casualties, but more importantly was rendered ineffective as a

ON THIS SITE STOOD THE SMITHY OF WILLIAM SKELHORN AT WHICH QUEEN MARGARET HAD HER HORSE'S SHOES REVERSED TO AID HER ESCAPE FROM THE BATTLE OF BLORE HEATH 23ʳᵈ SEPTEMBER 1459.

fighting force for the time being. Salisbury was able to push on to Ludlow and join up with his allies. From there, the combined force began a march towards Worcester.

Below: Ludlow castle was taken by Lancastrian forces in 1459, but remained a possession of the Duke of York's family. Edward IV sent his son, Edward, to Ludlow to be raised, and it was from here that he set out for London to be crowned.

Yorkist Disaster at Ludford Bridge

By October 1459, Richard of York had concentrated with his allies at Ludlow. He marched towards London but became aware of a greatly superior royal force moving to intercept him. After a brief stop at Worcester, York retired towards the town of Ludford, which was associated with his castle at Ludlow. He sent the usual messages of loyalty and

Above: The battle of Ludford Bridge was decided when part of the Yorkist force changed sides. As the Yorkist army collapsed, its leaders fled and ultimately found refuge in Calais and Ireland. They were attainted by Parliament in their absence.

support to King Henry, perhaps hoping for another negotiated settlement, but the time for this had passed.

York was presented with a serious problem at this juncture. It was one thing to skirmish with lords who were loyal to the circle of favourites around Henry, and quite another to raise arms against the king himself. Whilst the conflict had been presented as a loyal attempt to remove bad advisors from around the throne and to free the king of their influence, many had been willing to fight. Now the king himself was in charge of the army approaching Ludlow, and it was questionable how many of York's troops would be willing to fight against him.

York established a defensive position with the river to his front, covering the approaches to the bridge with cannon, but confidence was low among his supporters. The final blow to Yorkist hopes came when a detachment of the garrison of Calais went over to the royal army. The Yorkist leaders waited until nightfall and quietly slipped away, leaving their troops to their fate. In the event that fate was quite merciful, although the town was plundered. Deserted by their commanders, the Yorkist force surrendered and was granted a royal pardon. York's wife and his youngest children were captured but not ill-treated. York himself escaped via Wales, eventually reaching Ireland, whilst Warwick and Salisbury fled by ship to Calais.

RICHARD NEVILLE, EARL OF WARWICK, 'KINGMAKER'

RICHARD NEVILLE WAS born in 1428 into the powerful Neville family whose main holdings were in northern England. His father, also called Richard Neville, was a younger son of the Earl of Westmoreland, but became an earl in his own right when he married Anne, Countess of Salisbury. This made the young Richard Neville heir to the Salisbury earldom, and by his own marriage he inherited the earldom of Warwick. He became Earl of Warwick in 1449, and is generally known by that title even when referring to events before his assumption of it.

Neville's new connections with Warwick created conflict with the Beaufort family, which also stood to inherit some of the same lands through marriage, and his family were also involved in a lengthy feud with the Percys. The young Neville sided with Henry VI in 1452 when Richard of York made his first challenge, but subsequent events pushed him into the Yorkist camp.

Continuing rivalry with the Beauforts was made worse by the grant of lands to them that Neville also claimed. The Beauforts were favourites at court and used their influence to the detriment of others, particularly after Henry

VI was incapacitated by madness in 1453. As the Beauforts were eclipsed and Richard of York took over as Lord Protector, Warwick was a powerful supporter of his faction.

Warwick's appointment as Captain of Calais increased his personal power even further, enabling him to act as 'kingmaker' in the later stages of the Wars of the Roses. By 1462, he was the richest and most powerful man in the country other than the king – and arguably wielded more influence than the king even if he had less direct power.

After the accession of Edward IV, Warwick's power was so great that for a time he had both Henry VI and Edward IV imprisoned and under his control. However, events turned against him and he was forced to flee to the Continent where he forged an unlikely alliance with Margaret of Anjou.

Attainted by Parliament in 1470, Warwick finally met his downfall at the Battle of Barnet in 1471, when he was killed trying to escape the collapse of his forces. Even after this, the division of his lands and holdings caused disputes that culminated in a clash between Richard of Gloucester (Richard III) and the Duke of Clarence.

Left: Richard Neville's influence on English politics was far-reaching. His disputes became one of the factors that shaped the course of the Wars of the Roses, whilst his use of crown appointments to enrich himself caused tension with foreign powers.

Henry VI summoned Parliament, which met on 20 November. This session became known as the Parliament of Devils, as its purpose was to pass bills of attainder against the Yorkist leaders. A bill of attainder was a Parliamentary act declaring individuals guilty of treason or some other serious crime without a trial being held. There was no chance of the latter; the Yorkist leaders were never going to present themselves for judgement in front of a hostile court.

The Yorkist leaders were all judged to be 'attainted', and thus forfeited all their rights, titles and properties. These would pass to the crown rather than being inherited in the normal manner. Those attainted by Parliament on this occasion were Richard of York and his eldest sons Edward and Edmund, as well as the Earls of Warwick and Salisbury, both of whom were named Richard Neville.

The Parliament of Devils theoretically stripped the Yorkist leaders of all their property and their ability to raise funds or troops. However, if the Lancastrian faction succeeded in alienating enough of the remaining nobility then the Yorkists might still be recognized as leaders against the crown. For the time being that was unlikely; Henry VI had apparently dealt with the opposition to his reign and was in a secure position. However, there were many who grew concerned over the severity with which the Yorkists were treated, especially since the court was dominated by Henry's favourites who were not above using legal process to get what they wanted. Those that were not in favour, or who lacked the power to oppose the circle of favourites, were uneasy since without the Yorkist counterbalance there was nothing to stop them doing whatever they wanted.

Right: The Battle of Northampton was a decisive Yorkist victory, brought about at least in part by treachery. The defection of Lord Grey de Ruthyn compromised an otherwise very strong position and allowed the Yorkists to once again capture Henry VI.

Hostilities Continue

Warwick reached Calais just ahead of Henry Beaufort, Duke of Somerset, who had been sent to take over from him. The garrison of Calais remained loyal to Warwick and repelled Somerset's attempt to take control of the port. His position was sufficiently secure that he was able to send a fleet to attack Sandwich.

There, Richard Woodville, Earl Rivers, was positioned to defend against exactly such an attempt. Despite this, Rivers was captured and his force defeated, after which Warwick sailed to Ireland, where Richard of York was at that time rallying support for his cause among the Irish nobility. Like Warwick, York had succeeded in repelling the Lancastrian leader sent to replace him. In York's case it was the Earl of Wiltshire.

Warwick and York agreed on a plan of action and in June 1460, Warwick returned to England at the head of a force from Calais. With him were the Earl of Salisbury and Edward, Earl of March. They landed at Sandwich and marched on London, gathering support along the way. There was little opposition at London, where Warwick was still popular as a result of his victories against the French and his support for the merchant class, as the king was in Coventry at the time.

In July 1460, a Yorkist army under the command of Warwick and Edward, Earl of March, met the royal army at Northampton. The Lancastrian army, commanded by the

Below: Upon the collapse of Lancastrian forces at Northampton, brave and loyal men, including several great nobles, gave their lives in a last attempt to cover the king's retreat. Henry VI failed to move quickly enough, rendering their sacrifice meaningless.

THE LOVEDAY AGREEMENT

AFTER LONG AND difficult negotiations, the terms of the Loveday Agreement were drawn up. Most of the terms were financial, offering a cash settlement for injustices received or claimed. Many of the terms were intended to reduce tensions in the realm; the Percy-Neville feud was a particular target of the agreement.

Under both a financial bond and a solemn oath, Lord Egremont (of the Percy family) was bound to remain at peace with the Nevilles for ten years. The Earl of Salisbury, on the Neville side, was required to withdraw fines imposed on Lord Egremont. The Yorkist faction was required to pay for a chantry at St Albans Abbey, where prayers would be said for those slain in the battle. The Lancastrians were to accept this as recompense for the deaths of their relatives and not seek vengeance.

Among the financial settlements was an agreement that the Earl of Warwick was to pay the Clifford family 1000 marks, whilst Richard of York was required to give 5000 marks to Somerset. Since he was owed a great deal of money by the crown and thought it likely that he would never see it, York transferred part of the royal debt to Somerset rather than actually handing over any money. Whilst hardly in the spirit of the Loveday Agreement, this action serves as an example of how it was regarded by most of those involved. Although the Yorkist and Lancastrian leaders walked arm in arm behind Henry VI to St Pauls' Cathedral, within months they were once again fighting for control of his realm.

Duke of Buckingham, had established a fortified position covered by cannon, but these were unserviceable due to heavy rain on the day of the battle. Not only had part of the Lancastrian defence been nullified by rain, a greater part was taken out of the fight by treachery. The Lancastrian left flank, commanded by Lord Grey, stood aside and allowed the advancing Yorkists to enter their positions. Lord Grey had been promised support in his own disputes as well, possibly, as a senior office in government. This piece of treachery allowed the Yorkists to breach the Lancastrian defences with ease.

Although compromised, the remaining Lancastrian forces put up a stiff fight. The Duke of Buckingham died trying to prevent the Yorkists approaching the king, as he had promised to do before the battle. Several other nobles were slain, but bloodshed was limited by an order from Warwick to spare any common soldier who laid down his arms. The king was captured in his tent, and escorted to London with great courtesy. There they were joined by Richard of York, who had returned from Ireland with forces of his own.

The Act of Accord

Parliament was called in October, and at this time Richard of York pressed his claim to the throne by laying his hand upon it. This caused division among the nobility – ousting Henry's corrupt circle of advisors was a different matter to deposing the king. York was asked why he was making his claim at this point yet had not before when he had the chance, and responded that his right might lie silent but would not expire or diminish.

However, Parliament was not willing to accept usurpation of the throne. Chief among those seeking a negotiated settlement was Warwick, who may or may not have known about York's plan to seize the throne from their meeting in Ireland. Whether he did or not, he would not support the claim when the time came, forcing a new round of negotiations.

The result was the Act of Accord, an agreement whereby Henry VI would reign for

> 'The stakes were continually being raised, with the factions increasingly intolerant of those who tried to stay on the sideline'.

the remainder of his life but the crown would then pass to Richard of York. This disinherited the young Prince Edward, which was totally unacceptable to Margaret of Anjou. Many other Lancastrian supporters agreed, creating a situation where the Yorkists controlled London and the king but much of the rest of the country was opposed to them.

This situation was in some ways a reverse of that prevailing at the outbreak of hostilities, but the similarity is at best superficial. Much had changed over the past few years, with what had been a dynastic and territorial dispute evolving into a series of blood feuds between noble houses. The stakes were continually being raised, with the factions increasingly intolerant of those who tried to stay on the sidelines.

Left: Sandal Castle was positioned to be a useful base when Margaret of Anjou raised an army in the north of England. From here Richard came out to give battle at Wakefield and was killed when his army was decisively defeated.

The Battle of Wakefield

Margaret of Anjou had no intention of accepting Richard of York as heir to the throne, and sought assistance from James III of Scotland. Meanwhile Lancastrian forces were gathering in the West Country, Wales and the north of England.

Leaving Warwick to hold London and ensure the king remained under Yorkist control, York sent his son Edward to deal with troubles in the west while he marched north on 9 December 1460. Accounts vary as to the size of his force; he may have intended to raise more men along the way or could have simply underestimated the level of opposition he faced.

On 16 December, York's force encountered its first opposition. A Lancastrian force under the command of Edmund Beaufort (later the Duke of Somerset), on its way north to join up with other Lancastrian supporters, was encountered near Worksop. Accounts of the action vary, but it seems to have been a fairly small skirmish and York's force was not prevented from marching north. On the 21st, York's army halted at Sandal Castle near Wakefield. Lancastrian forces were encamped at Pontefract, and these were powerful enough to repel York's initial reconnaissance attempts. He sent messengers to request reinforcements but then chose to attack before any could arrive.

This was perhaps due to a poor supply situation. The march north had consumed

a large proportion of the army's supplies, and more were hard to find on the road in December. York may have decided to chance a battle because the alternative would be to retreat in a few days for lack of food. He may also have been concerned about becoming besieged if the enemy continued to receive reinforcements, or he may simply have been overconfident.

There are also claims that York was deceived by false banners into thinking that reinforcements had arrived, and so came out to fight in order to join up with them, and that he did not intend to fight at all. It is also possible that York was mounting a foraging expedition that ran into Lancastrian troops, bringing about an escalating clash in which his army was badly outnumbered. According to some accounts, a segment of the Lancastrian force advanced towards Sandal

Right: The spot where Richard, Duke of York, was killed in the fighting at Wakefield is commemorated by a monument. His title had given an identity to his faction, but soon after Richard's death the factional lines would become quite blurred.

Above: The victors at Wakefield were not gracious. Richard's head was displayed on the walls of York, wearing a paper crown. This was probably intended to demoralize the remaining Yorkists, but no collapse of morale occurred.

castle to tempt York out. The estimate of its size suggested he could defeat it, but once battle was joined, other parts of the Lancastrian army closed in and overwhelmed York's force.

Richard of York was killed in the fighting. His son Edmund of Rutland attempted to escape but was caught. He attempted to bargain for his life, offering a ransom, but was killed anyway. The Earl of Salisbury was captured soon after the battle, but was initially permitted to negotiate a ransom. However, he fell into the hands of commoners who had a grudge

against him and was put to death. This was not an uncommon situation in the era; noblemen had much to gain by observing the courtesies and customs of ransom, but commoners were not protected by such a system and stood to gain little from sparing a nobleman – they were unlikely to receive any part of a payment made for his life.

The head of Richard of York, wearing a paper crown, was displayed at York along with those of Salisbury and Rutland. After this the Lancastrian army marched southwards towards London. However, the Yorkist cause was anything but lost. The capital and the king remained under the control of Warwick, whilst Edward, Earl of March, inherited his father's claim to the throne of England.

HERALDRY AND OTHER SYMBOLS

THE PRACTICE OF using symbols to denote the identity of nobles or men-at-arms probably dates from the reign of Henry I or earlier, and seems to have been widely adopted by 1150 or so. Heraldic designs began as fairly simple lines and shapes emblazoned in contrasting colours, usually on a shield, to help combatants distinguish friend from foe.

This was important in an age before uniforms and other distinguishing marks, and did more than help prevent 'friendly sword' incidents. Being identifiable enabled a knight or lord to rally his friends and allies, and helped ensure that his deeds on the battlefield were noted. Social status was linked to prowess at arms, so it was important that others could not dispute who had performed which deed. Not surprisingly, bright and contrasting colours – actually, colours and 'metals' – were used to ensure that designs stood out enough to be recognizable through a helm eyeslits amid a chaotic battle.

Terminology developed to describe the increasingly complex heraldry of Europe, which continued to fulfil its original purpose of battlefield identification but also grew to have wider meanings. Heraldic symbols denoted first, second and younger sons of a household, and rules developed for combining heraldic devices when major families married.

Heraldry became incorporated into decoration and was used to identify holdings or retainers of an important household, creating something close to a corporate identity. A related trend was the increasing use of emblems by commoners associated with a noble house. Merchants and craftsmen, as well as townsmen and even labourers, began to display the badge of the noble house to whom they owed allegiance. Most famous of these badges were of course the red and white roses of Lancaster and York. These were not heraldic symbols but were a sign of identity and loyalty used by the supporters of both factions.

Left: The red and white roses were symbols used by tradesmen, servants and other followers to denote their affiliation with the houses of York and Lancaster. They were not battlefield banners nor factional symbols at the time of the conflict.

RED ROSE OF THE HOUSE OF LANCASTER   **WHITE ROSE OF THE HOUSE OF YORK**

EDWARD, EARL OF MARCH

During his time as Lieutenant of France, Richard of York's wife Cecily Neville was with him at Rouen when she gave birth to a son. The boy was named Edward, and although he was their second son he was the first to survive to adulthood.

◆

'As a prisoner Henry was deprived of freedom and control'.

E dward thus became the seventh Earl of March, which was the most senior of the Duke of York's lesser titles, and was heir apparent to the Duchy of York. He also inherited his father's claim to the throne as a descendent of Edward III. Leadership of the Yorkist faction devolved on Edward in 1460, after the Battle of Wakefield in which his father and younger brother Edmund were killed. Edward was at this time campaigning in the

Edward, Earl of March, entered London in February 1461, where he was received favourably by the population. He was crowned on 4th March 1461, even though the Lancastrian army nominally commanded by Henry VI still posed a significant threat.

west of the country against Lancastrian forces there, while the Earl of Warwick held London.

Henry VI was imprisoned in London during this period, although he was still king in name. The Lancastrian goal was to free the monarch and drive the Yorkists from London; Edward and his forces in the west were less of a priority. This reflected the importance of symbols as much as economics in the era; London was the centre of the English economy and holding it gave financial advantages, but just as importantly it was symbolic of control. The faction that held the seat of government not only had access to easier administration, but also would gain support by being seen to be in control.

It was likewise with the person of the king. Control of the king made it possible to force him to agree measures that might otherwise not

EDWARD, EARL OF MARCH

EDWARD, LATER EDWARD IV of England, was born in Rouen in 1442, whilst his father was Lieutenant of France. He was the first Yorkist King of England and one of the few kings to be deposed and then regain his throne. He also achieved the distinction, rare during the Wars of the Roses, of living long enough to die of natural causes.

Edward was tall and handsome, with a manner that many considered made him likable, but he was not as easily led as Henry VI. With that, and also due to his very considerable abilities as a warrior, he was an excellent candidate for the crown. Edward was the seventh Earl of March, and inherited the title of Duke of York upon the death of his father, Richard of York, in battle at Wakefield in 1460. Edward also inherited his father's claim to the throne of England. He had no option to stay out of the Wars of the Roses even if he wanted to; his claim to the throne made him potentially dangerous to Henry VI and his supporters, who were sure to imprison or perhaps execute Edward if they gained control over him.

Edward was crowned as Edward IV in 1461, whilst Henry VI was imprisoned. The Lancastrian faction had already been dealt some serious blows, and Edward IV continued to suppress opposition after his coronation. However, his preference for following his own wishes rather than those of Richard Neville, Earl of Warwick resulted in a rift between king and kingmaker that led to open conflict. Edward was imprisoned for a time but released in 1469.

Further conflict between Edward VI and Warwick resulted in the restoration of Henry

Above: The seal of Edward IV. Edward's reign appeared to be an island of stability in turbulent times, but although his kingdom seemed fairly secure against the Lancastrian threat, his policies alienated former Yorkists.

VI to the throne and the flight of Edward to the Continent, where he was granted support by the Duke of Burgundy. This enabled Edward to return to England and rally further support. Edward defeated Warwick in battle at Barnet in 1471, where the kingmaker was killed.

Edward IV resumed his throne, and found himself secure enough to campaign against France in 1475 and Scotland in 1482. He died in 1483, and was briefly succeeded by his son Edward. However, the 12-year-old prince was intercepted on his way to London and imprisoned by Richard, Duke of Gloucester, who then assumed the throne as Richard III.

Above: Henry VI displayed a rare talent for being captured by his enemies. It is not clear exactly why his enemies kept him alive when so many others were executed, but this did allow Warwick to use Henry as a figurehead during 1470–1.

be passed, but it was also a symbol of who was really in control of the kingdom. The division of the country into factions was well known, and events like the capture or release of the king would make one side or the other seem much stronger. This would help sway wavering supporters or even fairly neutral observers towards the Yorkist or Lancastrian camp.

The Second Battle of St Albans

Having defeated and killed Richard of York at Wakefield in December 1460, the Lancastrian faction could be forgiven for thinking that the tide had turned. However, London remained in the hands of the Yorkists, and so did the king. Led by Margaret of Anjou, the Lancastrian

Above: Victory at the second battle of St Albans enabled Margaret of Anjou to free her husband from captivity, but the military advantage she gained was short-lived. Failure to seize London handed the initiative back to the Yorkists.

> 'The seizure of St Albans would place the Lancastrian force on Warwick's flank, but they did not find the town undefended'.

force marched southwards with the intent of retaking the capital and liberating Henry VI from captivity.

The Lancastrian army numbered around 15,000 men and had an additional advantage in that Andrew Trollope had joined them. Trollope was a former commander of the Earl of Warwick's forces, leader of the contingent from Calais that deserted during the battle at Ludford. Trollope brought with him experienced fighting men, seasoned from their defence of Calais against the French, but just as importantly he knew Warwick's thinking. Another former Yorkist aiding the Lancastrian force was Sir Henry Lovelace, who had been captured at Wakefield and subsequently released on the condition that he would change allegiance. The information he provided allowed the Lancastrian army to quickly reach Dunstable, avoiding contact with other Yorkist forces in the area, and rapidly capture it.

Dunstable was taken on 16 February 1461, after which the Lancastrian force made a night march to St Albans. This was probably at the suggestion of Trollope, who correctly predicted Warwick's dispositions. The seizure of St Albans would place the Lancastrian force on Warwick's flank, but they did not find the town undefended. The initial Lancastrian advance was met by archery from within the town and was forced back, but Trollope then led a flanking movement to cut off the archers from the remainder of Warwick's 10,000 strong

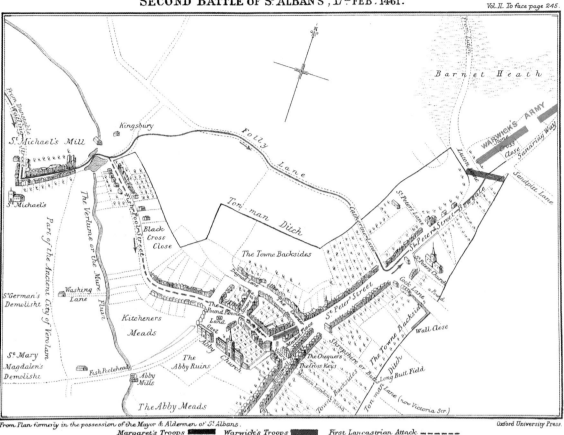

SECOND BATTLE OF ST. ALBANS, 17TH FEB. 1461.

Vol.II. To face page 245.

From Plan formerly in the possession of the Mayor & Aldermen of St. Albans.

Oxford University Press.

Margaret's Troops ▉▉▉   Warwick's Troops ▉▉▉   First Lancastrian Attack - - - - - -

Above: Lancastrian forces initially attacked St Albans shortly after dawn. They stormed up the hill, past the Abbey, where they were confronted by Yorkist archers who shot at them from inside their houses. This first attack was repulsed.

army. Fighting for the town went on all day, with the Yorkists gradually driven into a smaller area of the town and overwhelmed.

Support for the archers was slow in coming, not least because Warwick's commanders considered the attack to be a diversion, but eventually it became apparent that the main threat was not from the north. Warwick began to redeploy his army, which proceeded slowly. The nearest of his formations made an attack to relive the archers still fighting in St Albans but was repulsed. Some accounts attribute this to the well-timed treachery of Sir Henry Lovelace, who moved from supplying intelligence to openly fighting for the Lancastrians. Whether or not this was the case, Warwick's force was already outnumbered before this component was driven off, and was now in a very poor situation. This was made worse by wet conditions that caused hand-gonnes and cannon to malfunction. The only option was to attempt a withdrawal in the face of the enemy, which risked a total collapse of the army. Despite the difficulty of breaking contact, Warwick was able to extricate around 4000 of the 10,000 men he had started with from the fighting and move away. He was aided by the onset of night and exhaustion in the Lancastrian camp. Having marched all night and fought all day, the Lancastrian force was not in any condition to pursue.

Not all of the Yorkist host escaped. Some elements were cut off and unable to escape, whilst two knights in particular met a tragic fate. They were Lord William Bonville and Sir Thomas Kyriell, both distinguished and honourable men who had volunteered to

---

'Henry was apparently having another of his fits of madness at this time; many accounts record him as being unconcerned about the battle raging around him'.

---

protect the captive Henry VI throughout the battle. Henry was apparently having another of his fits of madness at this time; many accounts record him as being unconcerned about the battle raging around him. It was thus necessary to protect him as much as it was to prevent an escape. Bonville and Kyriell ensured that their charge was unharmed throughout the battle and the somewhat confused retreat that followed, and turned Henry over to the Lancastrians with due respect. In return for this courtesy, Margaret of Anjou ordered them put to death. Her son, Prince Edward (who was at that time around seven years old) was given the choice of method and chose beheading. The young prince was to display a curious fascination with beheading his enemies. It was noted as being one of his favourite topics of conversation when he was in exile in France, by observers who found him a rather disturbing young man.

Henry VI apparently recovered his senses sufficiently to knight a number of his rescuers, including Prince Edward and Andrew Trollope. After this the Lancastrian army pushed south towards London. There, they found the city's gates closed against them. The main reason for this was fear that the Lancastrian army would pillage the city. It had done plenty of pillaging on the march south, partly to obtain supplies and partly to maintain the allegiance of the Scottish contingent that had joined it. Many of these men were adventurers and mercenaries with no interest in the dynastic squabbles of England but a strong desire to fill their pockets whilst they had the chance. Although these warriors had added greatly to Lancastrian fighting capability their excesses now became a serious problem.

Unable to enter London, the Lancastrian force retired northwards, losing some of its Scottish contingent along the way. Most returned home; some slipped away to maraud more freely. This weakened the Lancastrian host just as another battle was in the offing.

Edward Returns

Edward, son of Richard of York, had been active in the west since the previous year. Wintering in Gloucester he raised troops, planning to oppose Lancastrian forces in Wales. Upon news of his father's death Edward began preparations to march to London but was forestalled by Sir Owen Tudor and the Earl of Pembroke, who were leading a Lancastrian army east out of Wales. Keen to prevent a junction of these new forces with the main Lancastrian host, Edward moved to meet them with around 2500 men. He was outnumbered by the Lancastrians, but their 3500 or so troops were not experienced.

Advancing to Mortimer's Cross, Edward's army witnessed what was presented to them as a good omen. A meteorological phenomenon known as parhelion (also mock sun or sun dog) made it appear that there were three suns in

Above: By the time of the battle of Mortimer's Cross in 1461, reprisals and counter-reprisals were commonplace after a battle. No mercy was shown to captured Lancastrian notables; among those executed was Owen Tudor, step-father of Henry VI.

the sky at once. Edward took this to represent his father's three remaining sons and he later used this image of the 'sunne in splendour' as his emblem.

The ensuing battle, which took place on 2 February 1461, opened like a reversal of Blore Heath. The Yorkist force could afford to remain in its positions, whilst the Lancastrians had to force a way past in order to meet the rest of their faction. Thus it was the inexperienced Lancastrians who attacked. After an exchange of archery, the factions clashed in a poorly-documented struggle that was ultimately won by the Yorkist force. Given the small size of the armies involved and the fact that the battlefield was constrained by the river Lugg and by woods to the west, it is possible that there was not much to document about this fight. With no clever manoeuvres possible and no real advantage on either side, the Battle of Mortimer's Cross was most likely a straight slugging match in which victory went to the side with the greatest staying power.

OWEN TUDOR

Welsh husband of Queen Catherine, the widow of King Henry V, was executed at Hereford in 1461 following the Battle of Mortimers Cross. Grandfather of King Henry VII, founder of the Tudor Dynasty, his severed head is said to have been placed on the top step of the market cross which once stood near this spot.

Left: Owen Tudor was the second husband of Catherine of Valois, whom he married in spite of an act of Parliament forbidding it. Although often at odds with the crown, he fought for the Lancastrian cause until captured and executed at Mortimer's Cross.

THE RONDEL AND THE MISERICORDE

THE DAGGER WAS a standard backup weapon for a man-at-arms, and was also carried by other types of soldier. A variety of designs were available, ranging from what were essentially tools pressed into service as weapons to specialized armour-piercing daggers.

The rondel dagger took its name from its cylindrical grip and circular pommel. Its stiff blade could punch through chainmail by pushing the links apart, but would not penetrate plate armour. A rondel could be forced through a gap in the armour, including the eyeslit of a helm, if the wearer were incapacitated or held down. Body weight, vigorous pushing or bashing the hilt with a heavy object would force the slim blade of the rondel through a gap in armour. Many knights died this way; dragged from their mount or downed with a

serious wound, they were dispatched by a dagger stabbed through a gap in armour or laboriously hammered through an eyeslit.

The misericorde was a similar weapon with an almost identical function, though it lacked the broad circular pommel and generally took a more aesthetically pleasing form. It typically had a blade of triangular section with no cutting edges. The misericorde was named for a 'mercy stroke' delivered to a desperately wounded knight, but was equally effective for killing an enemy as despatching a suffering ally.

Both weapons were routinely carried as a sidearm by knights, and various techniques of attack and defence were developed using them. Any attempt to use a knife in armoured combat was likely to involve grappling and wrestling, which was a part of the knight's training. The same techniques were used to defend against an assassination attempt made when the knight was not wearing his armour, whether with one of these specialist weapons or a more humble knife of another sort.

Right: Many knights were despatched with a dagger rather than sword or pollaxe, although more potent weapons were generally employed to put them in a vulnerable position. A short, stiff blade was more effective against armour than many other weapons.

This proved to be Edward's Yorkists, whose greater experience made them resilient in the face of heavy Lancastrian attacks. The Lancastrian force was driven off with unknown losses, and several nobles, including Sir Owen Tudor, were captured and put to death. After this Edward marched to London. In the interim Warwick was defeated at St Albans but was able to join forces with Edward and enter London.

Coronation and the Battle of Towton

Edward was crowned as Edward IV of England on 4 March 1461. Henry VI was still at large at this point, but those that had spoken in opposition to Edward's father Richard of York usurping the throne were now silent. Indeed Warwick, who had been the chief opponent of usurpation by Richard, was now the architect of Edward's accession.

There was little time for celebration, however. The Lancastrian army was weakened by the return home of its Scottish contingent, and lacked general support. This was partly due to the inability of a force under King Henry to enter what was at that time still his capital. With Lancastrian forces militarily weak and little popular support, there was an opportunity for Edward to smash them for good.

Edward IV led his army northwards towards where the main Lancastrian host was encamped at Towton near Tadcaster in Yorkshire. Initially the operation went well; Edward's advance guards were able to secure a crossing over the River Aire at Ferrybridge after catching the garrison by surprise. Then they in turn were caught the same way by a force under Lord Clifford that rushed out from Towton. With the crossing held against him, Edward might have

Below: The Lancastrian army positioned itself on high ground above the River Cock, behind a depression in the ground for protection. The clash resulting in almost 30,000 casualties.

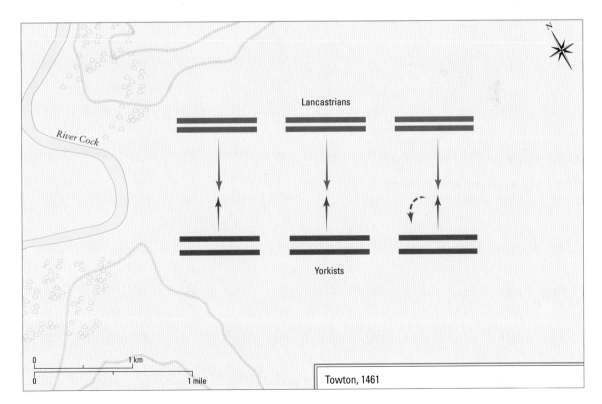

Towton, 1461

run into trouble had other elements of his force not managed to cross elsewhere and flank Lord Clifford's troops. He had no option but to pull back, allowing the main Yorkist army to make a crossing while their advanced elements pursued Clifford. He was brought to battle and killed in the ensuing defeat.

Edward's army then advanced on the main Lancastrian position, which was strong and apparently well-chosen. On 29 March Edward found the Lancastrians drawn up on high ground with a depression to their front,

> 'On 29 March Edward found the Lancastrians drawn up on high ground with a depression to their front, making an assault more difficult'.

making an assault more difficult. They also had the advantage of numbers – often quoted as around 60,000 to Edward's 50,000 – but were hampered by a snow storm blowing towards them from the direction of Edward's approach.

Edward led his army in person, assisted by Warwick and Warwick's well-respected uncle Lord Fauconberg. In contrast, Henry VI and his wife Margaret of Anjou were in York at the time, leaving the Lancastrian army to face the largest battle of the war under the command of Henry Beaufort, Duke of Somerset and Sir Andrew Trollope.

Although not all of his troops were in position, Edward opened the attack in the

Left: This depiction of the battle of Towton includes many of the tools of medieval warfare – the longsword, the mace, the dagger and the lance are all in knightly hands. The military bill, wielded by a humbler footsoldier, is also apparent.

usual manner, with archery. His bowmen had a distinct advantage, in that they were shooting with the wind, and the Lancastrians at times could not see their opponents to shoot back. Even when they could, driving snow and strong wind made their shooting less effective. Unable to tolerate this situation indefinitely, the Lancastrian force began to advance, hampered by the depression originally chosen for their own defence. The attack was uncoordinated, largely due to the difficult weather conditions and the rough ground, and was met with archery until the lines were close together. After this the Yorkist archers got out of the way and the infantry clash began.

Although things had not gone all that well for the Lancastrian force so far, it did have the advantage of numbers, and once hand-to-hand combat began, the issue was in serious doubt. The Yorkist line was severely imperilled, with King Edward personally rallying those nearby. The young king was a tall and imposing figure, and provided the sort of heroic leadership that was expected at the time. Edward was able to hold his army together through a long period of hand-to-hand fighting. Modern research suggests that the clash went on for as long as

Below: Skilful handling of archers greatly assisted in the Yorkist victory at Towton, although the issue was in grave doubt until the third Yorkist battle joined the fight. Its flanking attack broke the Lancastrian army and prompted a rout.

three hours before the remainder of Edward's troops arrived, led by the Duke of Norfolk, and attacked the Lancastrian flank. This decided the matter, and although the Lancastrians fought stubbornly for a time thereafter their line gradually began to collapse.

Escape from the battlefield was a difficult matter for the defeated Lancastrian force. Many tried to cross the River Cock at a narrow ford, creating a bottleneck that trapped a significant part of the Lancastrian force. Others were caught when they tried to break off in the face of the much less tired troops under Norfolk's command, or when bridges collapsed as too many men tried to flee across them.

Some sources claim that as many as 50,000 men died at Towton. Others put casualties at around 8000 Yorkists and 25,000 Lancastrians.

Right: The largest battle fought in England, The battle of Towton, is commemorated by a monument known as Lord Dacre's Cross. It is positioned where the Lancastrian line stood at the beginning of the encounter.

Given the usual size of an army in this era, the casualty rates are staggering, and were made worse by orders to give no quarter. Indeed, such was the nature of the conflict by now that some nobles and knights were specifically sought out to be put to death.

Victory at Towton gave Edward IV more or less complete control over England. Henry was still alive, but had fled with his wife to Scotland where he was joined by the surviving Lancastrian leaders. Many prominent Lancastrians had been killed in battle, crippling the faction to the point where it looked unlikely to recover. However, the conflict was not quite

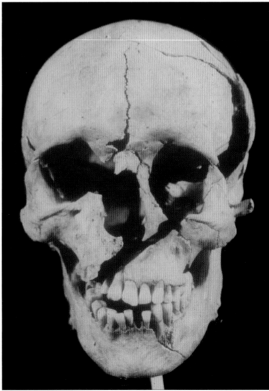

Left: Many of the Lancastrian casualties at Towton occurred when the broken army tried to escape. Struggling to cross the River Cock, Lancastrian soldiers were offered no quarter by their victorious foes.

Lancastrians were attainted, the majority of them had already been killed in battle. Some survivors, who refused to accept Edward's supremacy, were branded as traitors but even then he was willing to issue pardons to those who agreed to submit.

Several pro-Lancastrian strongholds remained even after this crushing defeat. The main Percy holdings at Alnwick, and other castles in the north of England, remained

Below: A skull found on the Towton battlefield shows a wound inflicted by a diagonal downward blow, probably with a sword. This warrior was facing his opponent; many of those slain that day were not.

over; Edward needed to consolidate his hold over his realm both militarily and politically.

After Towton

Edwards's actions after the Battle of Towton were less savage than those of many other leaders in the era. Although a large number of

defiant although their garrisons could do little more than passively resist Yorkist domination of the country. Henry VI and his main supporters continued their campaign as best they could with limited resources. Among these was Henry Beaufort, Duke of Somerset, who journeyed to France to seek assistance for the Lancastrian cause then returned to lead the resistance as best he could. Captured in 1462, he might have expected to be put to death but was instead pardoned and offered a position as military advisor to King Edward. This was one of several moves on Edward's part to try to reconcile former enemies, although in this case it failed. Somerset apparently gave good service to the crown from 1462–3, but then suddenly headed

to the north of England and began a rebellion against Edward. This brought about the Battle of Hedgeley Moor on 25 April 1464, when a force under John Neville, Lord Montagu, clashed with an approximately equal-sized army under the command of the Duke of Somerset. Montagu was on his way to Scotland for negotiations when he encountered Somerset's force. The Lancastrian wings collapsed, trapping their centre that was then smashed. However, Somerset and part of the Lancastrian force were

Below: Alnwick castle was one of the few major fortifications to remain defiant after the Lancastrian defeat at Towton. The Percy family continued to oppose Edward IV's rule, but the Lancastrian cause was fragmented and gravely weakened.

HEAD PROTECTION

THE HEAD WAS one of the most important body parts to receive protection, and also one of the most difficult to armour. Most areas of the body could soak up a certain amount of impact without too much damage, so a blow that did not penetrate would be survivable. However, shock transmitted through armour could still knock out or even kill a man-at-arms. Head protection had to do more than prevent penetration; it also had to disperse energy such that the wearer's head and neck were not subjected to enormous forces.

Numerous designs of head protection developed during the medieval era. The bucket-shaped 'pot helm' (also called the great helm, barrel helm and other names) completely covered the head and offered good all-round protection at the cost of reduced visibility and some difficulty in breathing.

Limited visibility was not too much of a problem for those used to wearing a restrictive helm; their senses adapted to a narrow field through practice. However, it did limit perception of the wider tactical situation. More importantly, breath was partially trapped inside the helm, meaning that the wearer was soon breathing partially-deoxygenated air. Coupled with the exertion of fighting in heavy armour,

Right: A bascinet helm, shaped to deflect blows from most angles. The curious pointed visor was developed to protect against arrows and lance thrusts, causing them to slide off rather than catch on an eyeslit or breathing hole and penetrate.

this could be exhausting. Some men-at-arms were known to remove their great helms during battle, relying on a lighter helmet worn underneath to provide added protection when the great helm was in place and hoping it would suffice when used by itself.

This was the origin of the bascinet, which evolved into a full helm in its own right. Early bascinets used an aventail of chainmail to protect the neck, while later versions often had an attached throat guard plate. The bascinet had a detachable visor, which could be raised to see or breathe better. The practice of raising the visor when approaching a superior eventually developed into the modern military salute.

Some men-at-arms preferred to leave the visor off their bascinet, trading slightly greater vulnerability for the ability to breathe more freely. This was a complex trade-off; a stray arrow or blow might hit the unarmoured face, but on the plus side the knight would tire less quickly and remain combat-effective for much longer, which in turn meant that he was less likely to receive a decisive blow.

The bascinet was gradually displaced by the armet and sallet helms, both of which continued to develop in terms of strength and shaping to deflect blows. The English sallet was typically worn with a large throat plate called a bevor, shaped to deflect blows away from the neck. The great nobility would tend to be equipped with the best armour and equipment, but lesser knights might be wearing helms of much older design.

able to break off and reach Hexham. Montagu then continued north to complete his mission.

Improved relations between Scotland and England would spell disaster for the Lancastrian cause, depriving its leaders of their safe haven and source of troops. They might even be handed over in return for concessions, and would likely have to flee overseas. The only answer was to win victories wherever it proved

---

'Montagu was not as inclined towards mercy as Edward and he ordered the senior Lancastrians executed'.

---

possible in the hope of reigniting support for the Lancastrian cause in England.

Edward IV marched north to crush this possible uprising, but Lord Montagu reached the main Lancastrian force, camped at Hexham, first on 15 May. Armies generally estimated at around 3000–5000 men on each side faced one another, with the Yorkists on higher ground. As they began their advance, a part of the Lancastrian army broke and fled. This left the remainder hemmed in by the river and unsupported. The Yorkist charge pushed some of their opponents into the river. Others were trapped and forced to surrender. Montagu was not as inclined towards mercy as Edward and he ordered the senior Lancastrians executed. Among them was Henry Beaufort, Duke of Somerset, although once

again Henry VI was not present at the defeat.

Henry's unfortunate habit of going mad in battles and getting himself captured might have prompted his supporters to keep him safely away. There was also the fact that he was not very good at fighting. This was a problem in an era where the senior nobleman present was expected to command an army in battle and to provide heroic leadership; neither of these were tasks to which Henry was well suited. Keeping him away enabled his supporters to keep their figurehead safe and at the same time place

Left: An incursion into England by Margaret of Anjou, who had taken refuge in Scotland, rallied Lancastrian supporters. These included the Percy family and the Duke of Somerset, who had come over to the Yorkist cause for a time. Ralph Percy was killed at Hedgeley Moor. Percy's Cross stands stands close to the battle site.

MARGARET OF ANJOU

MARGARET OF ANJOU was born in 1430. Her family, the house of Valois-Anjou, was related to the French kings and also had claims to the crowns of Naples, Sicily and Jerusalem. Although links to the French throne were by way of a cadet branch, i.e. through a younger son rather than direct succession, Margaret's family connections were sufficient to make her a desirable marriage prospect.

The marriage between Margaret of Anjou and Henry VI of England was arranged by William de la Pole, Duke of Suffolk, as one of several measures aimed at reducing tensions between England and France. Negotiations surrounding the marriage were long and complex, and involved England ceding territory to France. This made Suffolk highly unpopular when word got out, and attracted savage criticism from English nobles who believed that war, not conciliation, was the correct stance towards the French.

Although intelligent and attractive, Margaret of Anjou was also strong-willed and abrasive. She did not care about ruffled feathers among the nobility and did little to sweeten the harshness of her commands. She did, however, share her husband's passion for scholarship. Given that he was a gentle and easily-led man and she a forceful and determined woman, it is scarcely surprising that Margaret of Anjou became hugely influential at court. The royal wedding took place on 23 April 1445, and on 28 May Margaret arrived in London to great ceremony. She was crowned at Westminster two days later, and thereafter her influence increased steadily. The eclipse and subsequent death of Suffolk in 1450 allowed Margaret to come to the fore in court politics, and the birth of her son in 1453 cemented her position.

Margaret of Anjou was a staunch opponent of the Yorkist faction in politics and later in open conflict. She resented York's protectorate during her husband's illness, and intrigued against the Yorkists even while she was sidelined to care for the king. Margaret was the instigator of the great council of 1455, bringing about the first Battle of St Albans, and increasingly took the role of leader of the Lancastrian faction. Although not a field commander, she was the force of will that drove many actions, particularly those instigated by her husband.

To what degree Henry was a puppet of his

Left: Intelligent, beautiful but also somewhat arrogant, Margaret of Anjou was everything her hapless husband was not. She was the driving force behind the Lancastrian cause even when all seemed lost, continuing the fight despite being repeatedly driven from England.

Left: Margaret of Anjou was apparently able to find supporters wherever she went. Even in desperate flight with her young son, she was able to persuade robbers and criminals to assist her in escaping to continue the struggle.

when her son would ascend the throne. At the French court she made alliance with the Duke of Warwick, of all people, who was disaffected with the Yorkist faction. The two made a final bid for the throne of England but were defeated in 1471.

Captured after the Battle of Tewkesbury, Margaret of Anjou was well treated, spending some of her captivity in the custody of the Duchess of Suffolk, one of the first friends she had made upon arriving in England in 1445. She was eventually ransomed in 1475 and retired on a pension provided by the French King, although in return she gave up her inheritance rights to Anjou and her father's many overseas claims.

Margaret of Anjou died in 1482, having greatly outlived her son and husband. In an era of treachery and shifting allegiances, hers never wavered, although this single-mindedness might not have been in her own best interests. Abrasive and imperious, she was not open to compromise or conciliation, contributing to an all-or-nothing situation that ultimately led to her own eclipse and the demise of both her husband and her son.

wife remains debatable. Margaret was certainly quite capable of directing the Lancastrian faction whilst her husband was either mad, captured or both. Henry on the other hand did not seem to be able to go against his wife's wishes – after the second Battle of St Albans in 1461 Henry allegedly requested mercy for the knights who had protected him, and was overruled by his vindictive wife. Margaret was also capable of taking major decisions. She granted the town of Berwick to the Scottish throne in return for support against the Yorkists, and when this bid failed she fled to France but never stopped working towards the day

Above: Even without bouts of madness, Henry VI was simply too nice to be a king. He lacked the assertiveness required to impose his will on even a favourable court; he was completely lost in the savage politics of the Middle Ages.

an experienced and skilled general in charge, although at Hexham it availed them little.

The loss of his senior commanders forced Henry VI to take a direct role in operations against the Yorkists, leading to his capture at Clitheroe in 1465. He became once again a prisoner of the Yorkists, but was not executed. One possible reason for this was that while he lived any plot to restore the house of Lancaster to the throne would form around him, forcing his co-conspirators to deal with his madness and ineptitude. Similarly, if a plot did form then it would be around someone already in Edward IV's custody rather than an individual at large and free to raise support.

It is also possible that Edward, who was more inclined to be forgiving than many of his contemporaries, considered Henry to be harmless. Henry was a genuinely good and gentle man, more suited to being a scholar or perhaps a priest than a leader. It is quite possible that Edward did not want to destroy him unless circumstances forced him to. Henry VI might actually have been happier as a royal prisoner than as the leader of a nation at war with itself.

His bouts of madness were likely brought on by stress and the shock of bad news, neither of which had been in short supply. As a prisoner Henry was deprived of freedom and control over his own fate, but he was able to read and to pray, and to live free of the burdens of an office to which he was wholly unsuited.

Edward had apparently won the Wars of the Roses. His enemies were crushed, the former king was back in his custody and relative peace had settled over England. But, all was not well. His staunchest foe, Margaret of Anjou, was still free and plotting against him and divisions among former allies would soon result in a new round of conflict.

Right: Dressed up in armour and fearsomely armed, Henry VI could look the part of a martial ruler, but he could not act it. A king was expected to lead as well as command, taking bold decisions and implementing them violently.

·EDWARD·IV·

THE FIRST REIGN OF EDWARD IV

Edward IV's early reign was characterized by Lancastrian revolts despite his attempt to conciliate his new reign by winning over former enemies. Edward realized that if conflict was continued in the current manner it could only end with one faction reduced to powerlessness.

---◆---

'They would not be safe if they fell out of favour for any reason'.

The Yorkists were apparently in a position to achieve this in the early 1460s, if they chose to do so. They were in control of most of the country and, at least some of the time, held the former King Henry VI captive. Militarily, the Lancastrians were reduced to nibbling at the fringes of Yorkist power with raids and minor insurrections. There was still

Edward IV was a young man when he took the throne. Tall and good-looking, he had a manner with people that made him very likable, which worked to his advantage. His royal arms (above) comprising the emblems of England and France.

much support for their cause, but any noble who had not already openly declared for the Lancastrian side – and many who had but who were in a position to submit to Edward's rule – was well advised to keep his own counsel and await an opportunity to act.

Thus the only active opposition to Edward's reign was the hard core of Lancastrian supporters following Margaret of Anjou and her son Edward. Margaret had avoided capture after the Battle of Northampton in 1460 and fled to Harlech and then to Scotland where she obtained assistance for her cause. This came at the price of ceding Berwick to the Scottish crown. Margaret did not, initially, accompany the Lancastrian army and so missed the victory at Wakefield in December 1460 where the

Above: In 1462, Margaret of Anjou attempted to bring an army from France into England. Her fleet was struck by a storm, forcing her to come ashore at Berwick. Despite this setback, she continued to oppose Edward's reign as best she could.

'The early to mid-1460s were a time when the Yorkists consolidated their control over England but did not completely destroy the Lancastrian faction'.

Duke of York was killed. She rejoined the army in time for the second Battle of St Albans in February 1461, and was responsible for insisting that Yorkist captives be put to death. After the Lancastrian defeat at Towton in March of that year, Margaret, Henry and their son Edward of Westminster were forced to once again go into exile in Scotland.

The Lancastrian cause was not extinguished at this point. There were many who might rise up again if they saw a realistic chance for success, but as the Yorkists put down revolts and drove back incursions from Scotland, it was obvious that this was not the time. Further attempts to resume the offensive met with failure; Margaret obtained some French support for an attack on Northumberland in October 1461, which was modestly successful, but her supporting fleet fell afoul of the weather and she was almost killed.

By August 1463, Margaret of Anjou could do no more in England. Minor Lancastrian raids went on, but achieved little except to put her in personal danger. After a series of narrow escapes she journeyed to France and found safety for her son at the court of her father, René of Anjou. This took her out of the conflict for a time, which coincided with the period of greatest weakness for the Lancastrian cause.

Had Edward opted to crush his opponents completely in their time of weakness, he might have succeeded. However, that could have created new problems. The remaining nobility might be worried about a king who did away with all opposition, fearing that once his power became unlimited they would not be safe themselves if they fell out of favour for any reason. Edward may also have genuinely believed that it was possible to heal the rifts that had divided England by offering reconciliation to anyone who wanted it

Thus the early to mid-1460s were a time when the Yorkists consolidated their control over England but they did not completely destroy the Lancastrian faction. Richard Neville, Earl of Warwick, and his brother John Neville, marquis of Montagu, were instrumental in restoring order to the kingdom and preventing a Lancastrian resurgence. They also provided guidance to the young King Edward, which meant that the Nevilles essentially ran England.

Edward made a number of royal progresses around his kingdom during this time, fulfilling an important administrative and political function, while the Nevilles championed his cause militarily. This was a critical part of the king's duties and also helped restore confidence that stability was returning. Edward did take part in some of the fighting but was busy with affairs of state at the time of the Battle of Hexham that more or less ended the Lancastrian threat to his rule. This was probably the correct way to

Left: Other than a few occasions where it seemed necessary, Edward IV was willing to leave military affairs to his commanders and to busy himself with administering the kingdom. After years of civil war, there was much to attend to if stability was to be achieved.

go about ending the conflict. The young king had seen enough battle and acquitted himself sufficiently well that there was no question about his courage or abilities as a warrior. There was thus no real need to risk himself in battle when others could lead his armies as ably – the death of Edward in some skirmish could undo all the work done to date. Conversely, Edward could fulfil functions that the Nevilles could not – there was, after all only one king. England needed to be reminded about this, lest disaffected or ambitious nobles remember that Henry VI was still alive and begin plotting to support him.

'Warwick sought good relations with France, and was quietly negotiating a marriage between Edward and Anne of France, the daughter of King Louis XI'.

Conflict with Warwick

Had Warwick confined his activities to those of war leader and left affairs of state to Edward, matters might have gone differently. However, he was pursuing his own agenda, which included dictating England's foreign policy. Warwick sought good relations with France, and was quietly negotiating a marriage between Edward and Anne of France, the daughter of King Louis XI. Although she was a young child at the time, she was a desirable marriage prospect whose betrothal to the English king would bring about a powerful alliance and hopefully end French

support for the Lancastrian cause. Warwick's pursuit of this alliance was a usurpation of Edwards's powers as king, and was far beyond what any great noble was empowered to do without direct authority from the crown.

Right: Warwick favoured an alliance with France that would be cemented by marriage between Edward IV and Anne of France. Edward's subsequent derailment of this plan was one of the main sources of contention between them.

However, Warwick was so powerful at that time that he felt he could do as he pleased, including determining international policy and arranging dynastic marriages. His high-handed actions brought him into conflict with Edward, who had plans of his own. Edward favoured an alliance with Burgundy, which had long-standing disputes with the French crown, over close relations with France, and was increasingly exerting his own will rather than simply following the advice of the Nevilles.

Above: Elizabeth Woodville came to the attention of Edward IV when she pleaded with him to restore the inheritance of her children. There was little for Edward to gain politically from their marriage, but the Woodvilles gained enormously.

In one very important area, Edward's plans differed from those of his most powerful supporters. He was quietly pursuing marriage to Elizabeth Woodville, who was the daughter of Richard Woodville. A former staunch Lancastrian, Woodville had been elevated to

baron in 1448 for service to Henry VI. Now Baron Rivers, he fought for Henry and was captured trying to defend Sandwich against Warwick's expedition in 1459. Rivers had accepted the chance of reconciliation with Edward when offered, and joined Edward's cause. It is probable that Warwick felt no particular animosity towards him despite earlier clashes, but the secret marriage of Rivers' daughter Elizabeth and King Edward IV on 1 May 1464 was a potentially serious cause of division. Warwick had been promising the King of France a dynastic marriage with England via Edward, who suddenly took himself off the market with this action.

It has been suggested that Edward was seeking to make friends among the Lancastrians and their former supporters by marrying the daughter of one of their prominent captains, but this is unlikely. Elizabeth Woodville and her family were neither powerful nor wealthy, and Baron Rivers' connections among the Lancastrians were not greatly influential. It is more likely that Edward married for love. The marriage was kept secret for a time, and it was not until May 1465 that Elizabeth Woodville was crowned. In the intervening time the Nevilles had won the Battle of Hexham and reduced the power of the Lancastrian faction to almost nothing, and soon afterward King Henry was captured and imprisoned.

Elizabeth Woodville gave birth to a daughter, who was also named Elizabeth, in 1465.

Edward IV's mother, Cecily Neville, was displeased at the marriage and further offended by the naming of the first child. As the widow of Richard of York and mother to the king, she had been the foremost woman of the realm until her son married. She might have expected his daughter to be named in her honour, but instead he chose to favour his new wife instead. The Woodvilles rose rapidly as a result of the royal marriage. In 1466 Rivers was appointed Treasurer and soon afterwards elevated to an earldom. Other family members were given important offices, and soon the court was heavily under their influence. This irked Warwick, who had previously been on good terms with Elizabeth Woodville and her family.

'It has been suggested that Edward was seeking to make friends among the Lancastrians and their former supporters by marrying the daughter of one of their prominent captains'.

The Woodvilles opposed the idea of a marriage between George, Duke of Clarence and Warwick's daughter. Clarence was Edward IV's younger brother and had been appointed Lieutenant of Ireland in 1462. He was a close

Opposite: Elizabeth Woodville came from a family renowned for their attractiveness, and was considered the fairest of them all. Her large family were given positions of power around Edward IV, creating resentment among those less well favoured.

Above: Cecily Neville, Edward IV's mother, was displeased with her son's choice of bride and further offended when their first child was not named after her. Edward's marriage eclipsed his mother and greatly reduced her influence at court.

Above: George, Duke of Clarence, seems to have suffered from a treacherous nature. He betrayed his brother Edward in the hope of replacing him as king, then switched sides again when it became apparent that his allies intended to restore Henry VI instead.

associate of Warwick, and somewhat easier to control than his brother Edward. Indeed, when the rifts between Edward and Warwick deepened into open conflict, Clarence sided with his friend rather than his brother. Opposition to this marriage further alienated Warwick, who had hoped at one time that his daughter Isabel would wed Edward. When Elizabeth Woodville made this impossible, Warwick decided to settle for the nearest male relative to the throne but found this plan also opposed by the Woodvilles. The marriage went ahead secretly in Calais, in 1469, and for a while Clarence was a staunch supporter of Warwick's schemes.

In the meantime, rifts between Warwick and Edward IV grew deeper. Not only was Warwick edged out of his position of immense power at court, but he was made to look a fool when sent to negotiate a treaty with France in 1467. While Warwick was engaged in negotiations – and no doubt trying to explain to the disgruntled French king that his promise of a dynastic marriage had been derailed by actions of a king Warwick thought he could speak for – Edward decided that an alliance with Burgundy was more valuable than one with France.

Edward's treaty with Burgundy made Warwick's negotiations with France meaningless, and placed him in the difficult position of seeming to have negotiated falsely. He undoubtedly saw this turn of events as a personal affront. Warwick left the capital and retired to his estates for a time, then crossed over to Calais in 1469. There, after the marriage of Clarence and Warwick's daughter Isabel, he launched a campaign to regain control of England.

'A rebellion led by a man known as Robin of Redesdale began in April 1469. The exact identity of Robin Redesdale remains unclear'.

Warwick Invades England

Before leaving England, Warwick stirred up as much trouble for Edward IV as he could. A rebellion led by a man who was known as Robin of Redesdale began in April 1469. The exact identity of Robin of Redesdale remains unclear; he has been identified with two members of the Conyers family of northern

Opposite: Charles, Duke of Burgundy, was in conflict with France, whose nobility supported Margaret of Anjou against Edward IV of England. This was sufficient to cause Charles to side with Edward after he was deposed by Warwick.

CHARLES·IIII·DVC DE BOVRGONGNE AVPARAVANT
DE CHAROL

GEORGE, DUKE OF CLARENCE

GEORGE PLANTAGENET WAS born in 1449. He was the second surviving son of Richard of York, and was heir presumptive until his brother Edward produced a male offspring. Shortly after his brother was crowned, George was made Duke of Clarence, giving him the status and wealth appropriate to the king's brother.

Clarence was ambitious and apparently prone to treachery. Allying himself with Warwick, he joined in a plot to kill his own brother. While Edward was busy putting down a rebellion in Lincolnshire, his brother and the Earl of Warwick intended to attack his force with an army they had ostensibly raised to assist him. They must have intended to kill witnesses to their treachery as well; commoners' rumour-mongering could be dismissed but nobles who saw Clarence and Warwick turn on the king would have to be silenced.

The plot was exposed, forcing Clarence and Warwick to flee, but they soon returned to England and deposed Edward IV. This created a rift between Clarence, who expected to be given the throne, and Warwick, who instead freed Henry VI from captivity and used him as a figurehead instead.

Clarence was somewhat mollified by the agreement that he would inherit the crown as Henry's heir, but upon the return of Edward IV to England, Clarence changed allegiance again and sided with his brother. This may have been nothing more than self-preservation, but Clarence did fight against Warwick and benefited greatly from his defeat.

Left: The marriage of Isabel Neville and Richard, Duke of Clarence, was opposed by the powerful Woodville family. It was ultimately conducted in secret in 1469. Any censure that might follow was irrelevant by then – Clarence was actively plotting against his brother.

Married to Warwick's daughter, Clarence was able to claim his estates and titles, but by 1474 was in fierce dispute with his younger brother Richard, Duke of Gloucester. Gloucester planned to marry Warwick's younger daughter, which would give him rights to some of the Warwick estates. Clarence opposed this so vigorously that their elder brother, the king, had to intervene.

Isabel Neville, Clarence's wife, died in 1476. Clarence accused one of her ladies-in-waiting of poisoning her and used his power to ensure that she was convicted and executed. This was one of many abuses of power committed by Clarence, leading to suspicion that he was plotting to take the throne. Having already tried to murder his brother and take the crown once, it was not unreasonable to assume that he might try again.

Clarence made a bid to marry Mary, Duchess of Burgundy, for whom he had been proposed as a possible husband several years previously. The proposal was vetoed by King Edward, and soon afterwards Clarence retired to his estates. He apparently began plotting to take the throne, receiving oaths of allegiance from potential supporters and making preparations to raise an army. Such were the charges brought against him by

Edward IV, who personally led the prosecution of his brother. Treason and plotting regicide were always abhorrent to the crown, but when perpetrated by a brother they were even more offensive to Edward. Clarence was charged in January 1478 and a bill of attainder was passed. According to legend, Clarence was (presumably as a courtesy to his station as brother to the king) offered a choice of methods for his execution. He chose to be drowned in a butt of malmsey wine, which one can only suppose was the least degrading or horrific of the options.

Right: Having escaped retribution for earlier treachery, George of Clarence was finally sentenced to death in 1478. According to popular legend, he was offered a choice of methods of execution and selected drowning in malmsey wine. His other options are not recorded.

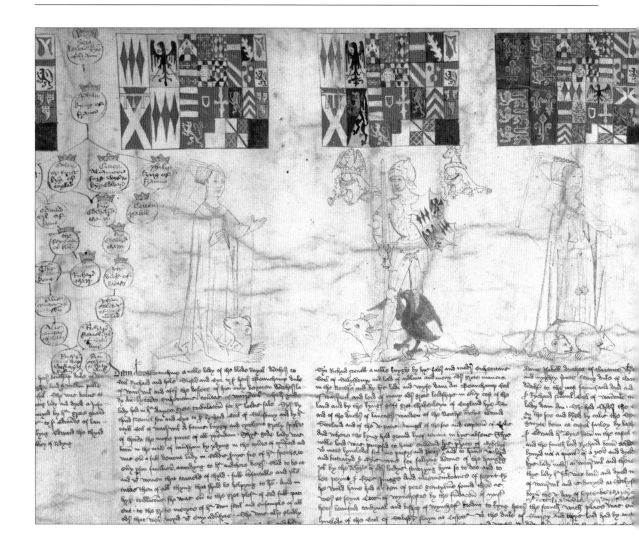

England. He may have been a composite figure or a notional figurehead intended to rally popular support behind an idealized leader, but in any case Robin was not the true instigator of the rebellion.

The revolt was fomented by Warwick, and not surprisingly the rebels demanded that the power of the Woodvilles at court be curtailed. Their published agenda followed a familiar theme – they stated that they only wished to remove bad advisors from around their king and to restore good governance. The rebels' manifesto dropped broad hints about the possible outcome of the situation by noting how previous kings had fallen as a result of surrounding themselves with similarly corrupt favourites. The rising was no rag-tag band of ill-armed peasants. Among its leaders were several members of the Neville family, though surprisingly perhaps the rebellion was opposed by John Neville – Warwick's brother – who was Earl of Northumberland as well as Marquess of Montagu. In fact, John Neville marched against a secondary rising led by Robert Hilyard, who proclaimed himself as 'Robin of Holderness'. This other Robin and his supporters wanted the Percy family restored to their previous power, which was a different agenda to Warwick's rising. It is thus less strange

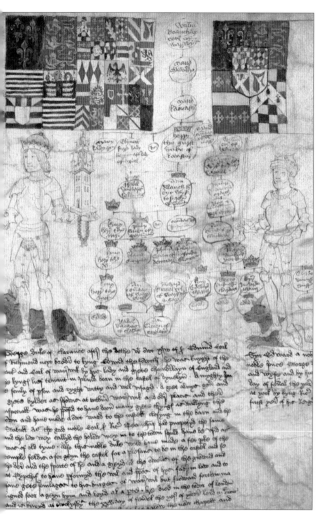

> 'Although a plan to marry Henry to William Herbert's daughter did not bear fruit, Pembroke was given custody of the future king for a time'.

a long and honourable history as a warrior. Pembroke had fought for Henry VI in France but joined the Yorkist faction when the country descended into civil war. He fought for the Yorkists against Jasper Tudor, the previous holder of the earldom of Pembroke, and remained loyal even when courted by the Lancastrian faction. As a reward for his service, William Herbert was given the earldom of Pembroke and other high offices by Edward IV. In 1468, Herbert had besieged his predecessor Earl of Pembroke at Harlech castle and upon its surrender captured the young man who would one day reign as Henry VII. Although a plan to marry Henry to William Herbert's daughter did not bear fruit, Pembroke was given custody of the future king for a time.

Pembroke was an opponent of Warwick, whom he suspected of being in secret correspondence with Margaret of Anjou, but was probably not aware of who was behind the rebellion in the north of England. What was known was that the rebels had declared support for Henry VI and were marching southwards. Pembroke raised an army and marched to join forces with the king.

With Edward in Nottingham, Warwick now landed in Kent with troops from the garrison

than it might seem that Montagu, although a Neville, opposed the rising. He wanted to retain his title as Earl of Northumberland and was quite willing to fight for it. Notably, he defeated Robin of Holderness' pro-Percy rebellion and killed its leader, but did not act against the larger Robin of Redesdale uprising.

In July, Edward IV marched to Nottingham in response to the rebels' movements. However, he had only a small bodyguard force and needed to wait for reinforcements that were summoned from elsewhere in the country. Among them was a force from Wales under the command of William Herbert, Earl of Pembroke, who had

Above: Sir William Herbert, Earl of Pembroke (see here with Edward IV), was an accomplished military commander. In 1468 he took captive Jasper Tudor and his nephew Henry (Henry VII) when he captured Harlech castle, but was executed after being defeated by Lancastrian rebels in 1469.

of Calais. This force was augmented by men from Kent, who rallied to Warwick's banner. He marched to London unopposed and occupied the capital. Meanwhile, the rebels moved to cut off king Edward from the armies marching to support him. Edward retired to Northampton, hoping that his loyal lords could join him there. This proved impossible. On 25 July Pembroke, whose force was composed mainly of spearmen, rendezvoused with other troops under the Earl of Devon. These were mostly archers – possibly

Left: Middleham Castle was a major possession of the Neville family. Richard of Gloucester (Richard III) and George of Clarence both lived there at times, and Edward IV was imprisoned at Middleham for a time.

as many as 7000 – which should have given the Royalist force a potent combined-arms capability. However, Pembroke fell to arguing with the Earl of Devon, who pulled his force out of the joint command and moved away, leaving Pembroke to face the full force of rebels alone.

> 'Exactly what passed between Warwick and Edward is not recorded, but Edward learned that he was not to be executed or even deposed'.

The rebels issued a challenge to Pembroke, offering battle near Edgecote, and he accepted without waiting for Devon and his archers to rejoin. Pembroke's force suffered badly from rebel archery, to which it had little reply, but was able to come to handstrokes. The issue was severely in doubt for some time, with Pembroke's brother Richard, armed with a pollaxe, apparently able to burst through the enemy line and back again twice in the course of a protracted struggle. The arrival of Warwick's advance guard made the battle unwinnable for Pembroke's force. He was captured along with his brother Richard; both were beheaded on 27 July. The king, meanwhile, was hastening to the area with a reduced force and arrived too late to achieve anything.

Edward had already dismissed the Woodvilles from his entourage, as he had been advised that their presence was reducing morale in an already fragile force. The victory of Warwick and his rebels at Edgecote caused all but the most loyal of Edward's remaining supporters to scatter, and these few were insufficient to protect the king. He was captured and brought before Warwick. Exactly what passed between Warwick and Edward is not recorded, but Edward learned that he was not to be executed or even deposed. He would remain king of England, although on Warwick's terms. Edward was taken in captivity to Warwick then Coventry, then finally to Middleham Castle. During this time Warwick technically had two kings of England imprisoned under his control. He used this period to secure his own position and to destroy his enemies.

Warwick's Rise and Fall
Warwick used his period of complete control to eliminate his enemies, the Woodvilles. The estates of Richard Woodville, Earl Rivers, had been plundered in 1468 by rebels sponsored by Warwick, and after the Battle of Edgecote he was captured at Chepstow Castle and executed at Kenilworth along with his son John. There was no pretence of legality about their trial and subsequent execution; Warwick simply ordered his enemies put to death. Humphrey Stafford, Earl of Devon, was also executed. This was on Edward's orders however, not Warwick's. Devon was blamed for the disaster at Edgecote, not without some cause – his 7000 archers could have made a big difference. He was apprehended in Somerset and put to death almost immediately on 17 August 1469.

Having secured his position as the power behind the throne, Warwick released Edward to take up his royal duties once again. It is likely that Warwick was finding it hard to govern the country without a king, and was apparently unwilling to depose Edward. The only option was to work with him and keep him under control. This had worked well enough in the past, before the Woodvilles gained power at court, so if Warwick could watch Edward carefully and avoid any repeat of the incident, he could continue to more or less rule England through him.

In the event, Warwick did not watch Edward closely enough. He was able to reassert his power and by early 1470 was in a strong position. Although relations with Warwick and with Edward's brother Clarence were outwardly good they continued to plot against the king. Unable to bend Edward to his will, Warwick sought to replace him with his more pliable brother. This of course meant that king Edward had to be disposed of. An opportunity became available – or was created – when Edward raised and led an army against a rebellion in Lincolnshire led by Sir Robert Welles. Welles was probably involved in a plot involving Warwick;

he confessed as much when captured and was in possession of incriminating documents. Welles was apparently disaffected with the appointment of Yorkist officials in Lincolnshire, and with the lack of Royal response to complaints about their actions. Welles also alleged that Edward IV was persecuting former rebels whom he had

Below: Earl Rivers, (presenting his book to Edward IV) unassailable when Edward was secure in his position as king, became vulnerable to Warwick's plotting once Edward was imprisoned. He was executed without trial.

EDWARD OF WESTMINSTER, PRINCE OF WALES

ALSO KNOWN AS Edward of Lancaster, Edward of Westminster was born on 13 October 1453. He was the only child of Margaret of Anjou and her husband, Henry VI. His birth displaced Richard, Duke of York, as heir presumptive.

Edward grew up in a time of great conflict and uncertainty, in which potential claimants to the throne might be executed as a precaution. Executions were a matter of state policy as well as a punishment for crimes, so it is perhaps not surprising that Edward became a little too fond of the idea of executing his enemies. His mother was a vindictive woman and his childhood was spent surrounded by an atmosphere of increasing mistrust and constant plotting.

Edward accompanied his mother during the initially successful Lancastrian campaign of 1460–1, which freed his father from Yorkist captivity but was ultimately defeated. After this he went into exile with her in France. It is not known what Margaret had to say about Henry to his son, but Edward's regard for his father cannot have been great. Much of his own misfortune – such as having to live in exile instead of enjoying the privileges of being a royal heir – were down to his father's repeated failures in battle and his lamentable habit of getting himself captured.

During his exile, Edward of Westminster developed into an imperious and vindictive man, who clearly believed in his birthright. He accompanied his mother to England in her final bid for the throne, in alliance with the Earl of Warwick. Warwick's forces were defeated at the Battle of Barnet on 14 April 1471, after which Edward IV and his brother Clarence led the royal army against the remnant commanded by Edward and his mother.

On 4 May 1471, Edward's force was confronted by the royal army and decisively beaten. Accounts vary as to how Edward met his death. Some claim he was brought before King Edward, who demanded to know why he had come to England. Edward of Westminster remained defiant and asserted his right to the throne, at which point King Edward ordered him summarily killed by his escorting knights.

In other versions of the tale, Edward of Westminster was captured by Clarence, who not long before had been his ally against the English King. Clarence held a brief and almost certainly illegal trial and put Edward to death by beheading. If this version of events is true, then his end will have come as no surprise to the young Edward of Westminster; beheadings were after all his favourite topic of conversation.

Above: Edward of Westminster was perhaps a product of his environment. His mother worked hard to ensure that Edward was not as ineffectual as his father, Henry VI, and ultimately succeeded in raising the boy far more in her own image.

Above: Edward IV's fleet was composed of the 'round ships' of the time. More suited to carrying cargo or large forces of men, these were not warships as such; naval combat was characterized by archery and boarding actions.

pardoned after the Battle of Edgecote. Whatever the truth of the matter, Welles had stirred up a significant rebellion and launched an attack on Gainsborough.

Edward IV first summoned the father and uncle of Robert Welles to court, demanding an explanation of these actions. They were subsequently pardoned but held whilst Edward dealt with the rebellion. At this time Edward received assurances from Warwick and from his own brother Clarence that they were raising forces to assist him. It seems that their real intention was to attack Edward whilst he was fighting the rebels, but this was forestalled by events. Edward demanded the surrender of Robert Welles and his rebel army, and when this did not materialize he had Welles' father and uncle executed. His royal army then crushed the rebellion in battle on 12 March 1470. The fighting was over quickly; many of the rebels fled when charged by Edward's forces, and the rebel commanders were captured.

Welles confessed to complicity with Warwick before his execution, forcing Warwick and Clarence to flee the country. They went to France, where they sought support for a bid to regain control of England. Clarence still believed that Warwick would make him king after deposing Edward, which had been the intention during the latest plot, but Warwick's plans were changing.

Warwick's Exile and Return

Warwick found sanctuary at the court of Louis XI. France was not well disposed toward England, and it suited the purposes of Louis XI to foment trouble for Edward. Further support came from the perhaps unlikely direction of

Opposite: Warwick was familiar with Louis XI of France, having spent time at his court trying to negotiate a dynastic marriage for Edward IV. The collapse of this prospective alliance left Louis willing to support Warwick in deposing Edward.

Margaret of Anjou. Her enmity for the Yorkist faction was very deep, and Warwick was one of its key leaders. Yet now their aims aligned at last – they both wanted rid of Edward IV of England.

Margaret of Anjou had never given up on her goal of seeing her son Edward on the throne of England. Her forays back to England from France had achieved little but to put her in personal danger, and from 1463 onwards she had dedicated herself to preparing her son for the chance that would someday surely come. For Edward's part, he grew up an arrogant and

'He and his mother were entirely ready to return to England and take the throne either in the name of a restored Henry VI or for Edward himself'.

rather frightening young man, who apparently talked as if he were a king and seemed obsessed with beheading people. He had been made in the image of Margaret of Anjou, an overbearing and imperious woman whose strong will had driven the Lancastrian faction for many years. He and his mother were entirely ready to return to England and take the throne either in the name of a restored Henry VI or for Edward himself.

Edward of Westminster, heir to the throne of Henry VI, was betrothed to Anne Neville, Warwick's daughter. This was a symbol of an accord between Louis XI, Margaret of Anjou and the earl. Support from France would put Henry VI or his Lancastrian heir on the throne of England – with Warwick in a position of great power behind the throne – and in return the English crown would assist in the ongoing dispute between France and Burgundy. Since

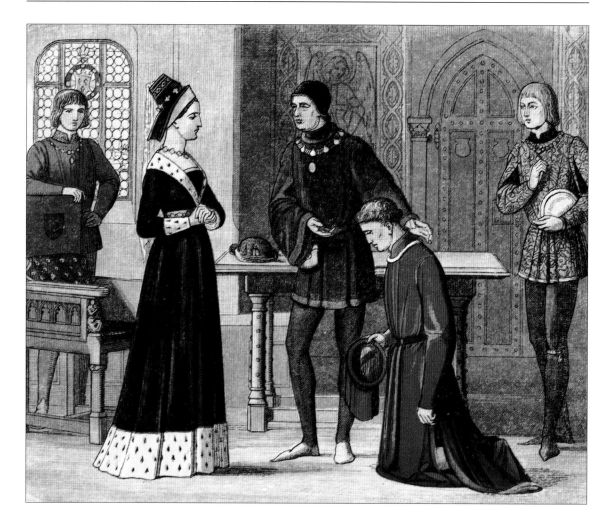

Above: By the later years of the Wars of the Roses, factional lines were very blurred. Margaret of Anjou, de facto leader of the Lancastrians for much of the conflict, made common cause with Warwick, one of her main Yorkist enemies.

Burgundy was allied to Edward's Yorkist faction, and that alliance had been the cause of great ill-feeling on the part of Warwick, these goals were acceptable to all.

Gathering other exiled Lancastrian lords to their cause, Warwick and Clarence landed at Dartmouth and marched on London. Caught unprepared and with little support, Edward IV in his turn took flight, finding refuge at the court of Burgundy. Edward's brother-in-law, Charles the Bold of Burgundy, made him welcome but at first did not offer any support towards regaining Edward's crown.

Margaret of Anjou and her son did not return to England when Warwick landed, but remained for a time in France. Thus, from September 1470, Henry VI was released from imprisonment by Warwick, who ruled England through him. This displeased Clarence greatly, as he had expected to be made king when Warwick triumphed. Instead he was sidelined and placed in a dangerous position as brother to a deposed king, heir to an apparently defeated faction and surplus to the requirements of those in power.

Above: Upon seizing power in England, Warwick released Henry VI from captivity. He expected to be able to run the country through a weak figurehead king in a way that had proved impossible when Edward IV was in his power.

METHODS OF EXECUTION

EXECUTION WAS A common punishment for a great variety of crimes in the Middle Ages, and was also used as an expedient in politics. Heirs to an estate or crown might become the focus for a plot at some point in the future, so a prudent and ruthless monarch might decide to rid himself of potential rivals if the chance presented itself. A noble might also be executed for other political reasons, such as if he had been given as a hostage as part of a treaty that was subsequently broken.

Executions were sometimes carried out on an *ad hoc* basis. For example, during the Battle of Agincourt in 1415 large numbers of French prisoners were taken – so many that they outnumbered their captors. When the battle looked like it was turning against the English, the order was given to execute all but the most senior (i.e. valuable) prisoners to prevent them taking up arms once again. The order was rescinded once the situation was restored but not before many men lost their lives. Executions of this sort would be carried out in a hurried and somewhat random way, with victims given a death-blow with whatever weapon was available – stabbed with daggers or hacked with swords and other hand weapons. Many would die slowly, or be finished off once the executioners had time to check who was dead and who was merely wounded.

Deliberate executions, rather than battlefield expedients, were carried out by a variety of methods. Some were bizarre and deliberately horrific, such as boiling. This could be quick, if the victim were put into hot water or oil, or extremely slow if the liquid was heated from cold. Other execution methods were based on what was available or the whim of the authorities authorizing the death sentence.

Some executions took the form of an assassination, with a captive attacked by surprise when he had no chance to defend himself. This might occur at any time after being imprisoned; however polite the gaolers, there was always the chance that they would be ordered to dispose of the prisoner. This allowed the captors to quietly dispose of someone they thought might be a threat or a burden in the future.

Left: Beheading with an axe was about the most merciful form of execution that a commoner could hope for. More commonly, victims were caused to strangle slowly whilst dangling from a rope in front of an amused crowd.

Left: A famous rebel's limbs might tour several cities or be placed on display somewhere prominent as a reminder that he had been defeated and killed. This would hopefully deter others from challenging those in power.

More commonly, an execution was a formal business often conducted with great ceremony. A noble, even one who was being put to death for treason or just being on the losing side of a battle, was someone to be treated with courtesy and respect. This helped maintain the social order, so even mortal enemies were often given a formal and rather polite execution. For nobles, the usual method was beheading with the sword. Executioners' swords were typically heavy-bladed weapons with a blunt point as they were not used for combat. Wielded in both hands, the sword could sever the neck and kill almost instantly and thus was considered relatively merciful. For non-nobles, the best they could hope for was beheading with an axe. This was also done on occasion as a mark of disrespect towards someone who might feel they merited a sword.

Hanging was the commonest method of execution. The relatively merciful neck-breaking noose was a relatively late invention, probably in the sixteenth century, and at the time of the Wars of the Roses death by hanging usually meant slow strangulation whilst dangling helplessly from the gallows.

For those convicted of treason, more brutal versions of hanging might be used, adding tortures including disembowelling or castration before hanging, or after the victim had been hanged until almost dead. Organs might be thrown into a fire after disembowelling, or the near-dead victim might be burned whilst still at least somewhat alive. Quartering, i.e. the removal of limbs to be displayed in various towns as a warning to others, might take place after death or be a contributory cause.

For a nobleman facing execution there was a last bargain to be made. If he played out the game to the end and met a good death, his family were less likely to be disinherited or otherwise punished for his actions. He was likely also mindful of the alternatives to a relatively painless beheading, and might make the choice to accept it as the least horrifying of a set of extremely unpleasant alternatives.

THE SECOND REIGNS OF HENRY AND EDWARD

Forced to flee England, Edward IV reached Holland in September 1470 and took refuge at the court of Charles the Bold, Duke of Burgundy. Charles the Bold was at odds with the King of France as part of a long-standing dispute, and was the ally Edward had sought in preference to Louis XI.

◆

'The 1468 Treaty of Peronne had resulted in a one-year truce'.

Charles the Bold was not initially receptive to the idea of supporting Edward's bid for the English throne. The reason for this was not least because he had major concerns of his own. Although the 1468 Treaty of Peronne had resulted in a one-year truce, the Burgundy–France conflict was flaring up again and Charles could scarcely

A hatchment is a display of the owner's heraldic components – the symbols he may use in his personal heraldry. That of Edward IV contains the royal symbols of both England and France, indicating his descent from the royal houses of both nations.

afford resources for an overseas adventure.

Charles the Bold had ambitions of creating a kingdom for himself, and had been adding to his lands by various means including purchase and treaty agreements. His military forces were also large, and they were unusually well disciplined by the standards of the time. However, his French enemies were very powerful and Charles could not afford to weaken his position without good reason. He had to consider the implications of a restoration of Henry VI to the English throne. He was not well disposed towards the idea of an England ruled by the wife or son of Margaret of Anjou, whose strong French connections would undoubtedly bring France and England into alignment against Burgundy.

Above: The treaty of Conflans, signed in 1465, yielded significant French territories to the Duchy of Burgundy. Within months a new conflict had broken out, with France successfully regaining territory in Normandy ceded by the treaty.

Continued good relations with England were more likely with Edward IV as king than with a Lancastrian on the throne. Charles was married to Edward's sister Margaret of York, and lending aid now would further cement good relations. That might prove useful in the future – although only if Edward succeeded in regaining his throne.

Thus Charles the Bold eventually agreed to furnish Edward with money and support. Numerous Englishmen were already in Charles'

service – he hired skilled mercenaries from wherever he could get them, notably England and Italy – and Edward was soon able to raise a small force for his expedition back to England. In the meantime there was good news. His wife, Elizabeth Woodville, had already given birth

Above: The marriage of Charles, Duke of Burgundy, and Margaret of York created close ties between Burgundy and England. Numerous obstacles had to be overcome, notably the interference of the French King who saw the union as a threat.

to three daughters but finally, in September 1470, she bore him a son. The boy was named Edward, and became heir apparent to the English throne. His reign, if it can be called that, was one of the shortest on record – he did not reach London to be crowned, let alone begin to wield power – after which he was deposed and spent his remaining life in the Tower of London. However, in late 1470 the birth of an heir seemed like a good omen for Edward IV, and in March 1471 he landed in England to reclaim his throne.

For his part, Henry VI was a figurehead for Warwick during this time. Margaret of Anjou was still in France, enabling Warwick to run the country as he pleased through a weak and biddable king. This was to Warwick's liking, but not so pleasing to Clarence, who had expected to become king. He began a reconciliation with his brother Edward, and agreed to support him if he returned to England.

Edward Returns to England

On 14 March 1471, Edward landed with his supporters at Ravenspurn near Hull on the Yorkshire coast; the same place that Henry IV had landed in 1399. He then marched on London and arrived to find it undefended. Edward remained popular in London, and had no difficulty in adding to his forces.

The decisive clash came on 14 April, which was Easter Day. Warwick's army was waiting at Barnet, drawn up on high ground near the town. Both sides deployed ready for a battle the next day, but Edward took the unusual step of redeploying under cover of darkness. He moved his forces stealthily closer to the enemy, either to give him the advantage of a sudden attack the

Below: Edward IV wrote to Francis II of Brittany, hoping to obtain assistance against his enemies. Francis had sided with Burgundy against France in the 1460s, but ultimately proved himself more friendly to Lancaster than York.

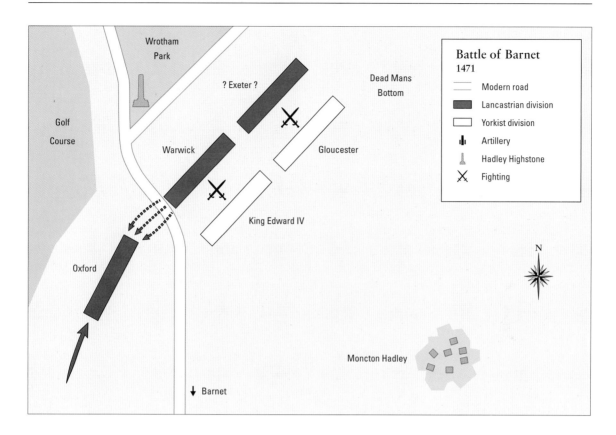

Wrotham
Park

? Exeter ?

Dead Mans
Bottom

Golf
Course

Warwick

Gloucester

King Edward IV

Oxford

Moncton Hadley

Barnet

Battle of Barnet
1471

——— Modern road

▉ Lancastrian division

▢ Yorkist division

▮▮ Artillery

⚑ Hadley Highstone

✕ Fighting

N

next morning or to ensure that Warwick did not break contact and move away during the night.

Warwick had no intention of doing anything of the kind. He had a good position and felt confident of victory. His artillery pounded the likely locations of enemy formations during the night, and Edward's guns replied. The science of field gunnery was not very advanced in this period. Even if the targets had been where the gunners thought they were, casualties might have been slight due to inaccuracy, slow reloading and general unreliability of the guns. Having moved his forces from their last known positions, Edward ensured that Warwick's bombardment did them little harm.

Dispositions for the battle were fairly typical of the times. Each army was divided into three battles, commanded by the senior nobles present. Edward's left, commanded by William, Lord Hastings, faced a Lancastrian battle under

Above: Edward's victory at Barnet was largely due to an over-zealous pursuit of his broken wing by troops under the Earl of Oxford. Oxford's returning men were mistaken for enemies; a 'friendly archery' incident escalated into panic and rout.

John de Vere, Earl of Oxford, and John Neville, Marquess Montagu. This force extended beyond Hastings' flank, giving an advantage to the Lancastrian host. The Yorkist centre was commanded by Edward IV and his brother Clarence. Edward probably wanted his brother close by to ensure that he did not betray him. The brothers might ostensibly be reconciled but Edward was not willing to trust his life to the promise that there would be no repeat of previous events in Lincolnshire. Clarence would have no chance to lead any portion of Edward's host against him if he were within Edward's personal command, but if assigned to one of the flanking battles he would have the right to command it due to his rank. Opposite Edward's central battle was a Lancastrian force under the Earl of Warwick. Some sources have this battle commanded by Edmund Beaufort, Duke of Somerset, with Warwick as overall commander or possibly associated with the leftmost battle, although there is doubt about this. Warwick was definitely present at the Battle of Barnet; Somerset probably was not. The Yorkist right, under Richard, Duke of Gloucester, was faced by a battle commanded by Henry Holland, Duke of Exeter. The positioning of the two armies was such that Gloucester's force extended beyond the Lancastrian flank, giving the Yorkist force the same advantage enjoyed by their opponents on the other flank.

> 'A long and evenly-matched struggle might result in surprisingly few casualties, but once pursuit began it often became slaughter'.

The Battle of Barnet

April 14th dawned extremely foggy, concealing the dispositions of both sides so that it was at first not apparent that both armies were exposed to a flanking attack. The centre battles on both sides engaged head-on and a struggle ensued, but on the flanks the relative positions of the armies produced a fairly rapid result. Gloucester advanced and began to envelop the Lancastrian flank, to which Exeter replied by pulling back part of his battle to meet the threat. Although hard-pressed his battle was able to withstand the attack; Gloucester's advantage was not decisive.

The opposite was true on the other flank. When the battle commanded by Oxford and Montagu began to lap around Hastings' flank,

his force disintegrated. Many of Hastings' men fled the field, pursued by Oxford. This had unexpected consequences, though for the moment the situation looked dire for the Yorkists. In most ancient and medieval battles, losses were much greater for the side that broke. A long and evenly-matched struggle might result in surprisingly few casualties, but once pursuit began it often became a slaughter. Undisciplined pursuit was thus not always a bad thing, as it ensured that the defeated side was well and truly scattered and would not be able to regain its strength quickly. It did, however, also take the pursuers off the field.

Historically, battles have been lost because of a local success that caused a part of the victorious side to take itself out of the equation. By the time the commanders rallied their forces, their absence might have been exploited by the enemy or at the very least some repositioning would have taken place to prevent exploitation of the advantage. A more disciplined force would pursue a short distance at most, then be available to attack the flank of troops exposed by the collapse elsewhere.

Thus Edward was fortunate that Oxford's troops chased his broken wing so far instead of rolling up his line with a flank attack. The benefits were much greater than that, however. Oxford and his men became badly disorientated in the fog and returned to the battle behind their own line. Had they fallen upon Edward's rear the battle would have been lost for the Yorkists, but instead Oxford caused a panic

Opposite: A depiction of the Battle of Barnet in typical style of the era. Whilst giving a good impression of the violence and savagery involved, such images are usually more representative of the general situation than accurate in terms of details.

Above: The Earl of Warwick was caught by his enemies as he tried to flee the field. Had he escaped, he might have joined forces with Margaret of Anjou, who was at that time landing in England with a new army.

EDMUND AND JASPER TUDOR

EDMUND AND JASPER Tudor were half-brothers of Henry V. Their mother, Catherine of Valois, was the widow of Henry V of England. In spite of an Act of Parliament forbidding it, Catherine married an obscure Welsh nobleman named Owen ap Meredydd, better known as Owen Tudor. They had five children before Catherine was sent to an abbey where she subsequently died.

Owen Tudor was imprisoned but escaped and was pardoned, and when Henry VI came to the throne Owen fought for him. He was captured and executed after the Battle of Mortimer's Cross, while his children were still very young. The eldest, Edmund, was born around 1430 and in 1453 was named Earl of Richmond. He married Margaret Beaufort, daughter of the Duke of Somerset, but died while she was pregnant with their only child.

That child was Henry Tudor, who would eventually reign as Henry VII. In the meantime he was protected by his father's brother Jasper, who was Earl of Pembroke. Such were the fortunes of the house of Lancaster that Jasper was stripped of his titles by Edward IV; they were given to his enemy William Herbert. Restored to the earldom in 1470, Jasper Tudor lost it again after the Battle of Barnet.

Jasper Tudor protected the young Henry Tudor and acted as a tutor to him, taking refuge in Brittany from Edward IV. He continually rallied support for the Lancastrian cause and was restored as Earl of Pembroke once again when Henry Tudor defeated Richard III (who at that time had taken the earldom as one of his titles) and took the throne as Henry VII. Jasper Tudor held high offices thereafter including Lieutenant of Ireland and Duke of Bedford.

Right: Owen Tudor was born around 1400, at a time when his native Wales was fighting English attempts to pacify its population. He was a cousin of Owain Glyndwr, who led the campaign against the English. This is the farmhouse near Pentraeth, Isle of Anglesey, Wales, where he was born.

Above: The Battle of Barnet is commemorated by this obelisk. Barnet was probably more significant than the following battle of Tewkesbury, in that the defeat of Warwick's army prevented a junction of forces with Margaret of Anjou and made a royal victory almost certain.

among his own allies. Mistaking the de Vere banner of Oxford for Edward's symbol, some of Warwick's archers began shooting at the force approaching them from the flank. The error became apparent after a while, but in that era treachery was always a possibility, and some among the Lancastrian force began to cry out that they were betrayed.

With an apparently hostile force in their rear, Warwick's men fell into confusion, enabling Edward's centre battle to push forward. The Lancastrian force then collapsed, with men fleeing the field as best they could. Warwick was killed trying to reach his horse to retreat, as was his brother Montagu. Henry Holland, Duke of Exeter, was also seriously wounded. Some accounts say he was rescued, some have him left

for dead but somehow recovering. Either way, he abandoned the Lancastrian cause and fled to France. His body turned up on the Dover shore in 1473, but it remains unclear how he died.

Oxford, too, escaped and made his way to France where he continued to champion the Lancastrian cause. In due course he returned to England with new forces to continue the struggle. In the meantime Edmund Beaufort, Duke of Somerset, was able join other Lancastrian forces under the command of Margaret of Anjou and her son Edward of Westminster.

Margaret and Edward of Westminster Return to England

Edward IV might well have thought the Lancastrian cause had been dealt its death-blow at Barnet. However, some Lancastrian forces were still at large, so he needed to act quickly to capitalize on this success. He did not know it at the time but Margaret of Anjou and Edward of Westminster had landed at Weymouth on

Above: Unable to reach their allies in Wales, Margaret of Anjou and her son Edward met the royal army in battle at Tewkesbury. Their defeat appeared to be the end of the Lancastrian cause and secured Edward IV's rule over England.

the very day that Edward won his victory over Warwick. They were soon joined by Somerset, posing a threat that could not be ignored.

Margaret's arrival in England had been delayed by storms in the English Channel, otherwise she would have joined forces with Warwick and the Battle of Barnet might have turned out differently. Now facing Edward's royal army without her allies, she considered retreating to France and waiting for a better opportunity. Edward of Westminster convinced her that the campaign was still winnable, or at least that there was no point in just turning around and sailing home, so Margaret resolved to fight it out.

Her best option was to move westward and join the forces raised by Somerset and John Courtenay, Earl of Devon. Courtenay was one of the Lancastrian lords who had fled into exile,

Right: Some Lancastrian leaders sought sanctuary at
Tewkesbury Abbey, but Edward IV seized them anyway and
had them executed after the briefest of trials. The abbey was
reconsecrated after this, as blood was spilled on holy ground.

and had ample time to conspire with Margaret
of Anjou during this period. He and Somerset
raised a very significant force, enabling Margaret
to mount a serious challenge to the royal army,
but more troops were needed. These could be
obtained in Wales, where Jasper Tudor had been
very active, or in the traditional Lancastrian
holdings of northern England.

Edward learned of Margaret's landing two
days after it occurred, but could not at first
discern her intentions. She sent forces out to
feint in various directions, concealing her real
direction of march, so it was a few days before
Edward IV could begin his move to intercept
her. Margaret had marched first to Exeter,
then to Bath, before heading north. A detour
via Bristol was necessary to obtain supplies,
but a foray towards Gloucester for the same
purpose found the city gates closed against the
Lancastrian army.

The Battle of Tewkesbury

Edward IV made an attempt to force a battle
at Sodbury, but was not in time to do so. He
pursued the Lancastrian army north as it
headed for Tewkesbury. Margaret's intent was
to cross the River Severn there, and to this end
she had marched her army hard. However, with
Edward's force in close proximity she was forced
to either turn and fight or risk being caught as
she made the laborious river crossing. There
was really no option, so the Lancastrian force
took up a position on high ground and camped,
trying to recover from the long and rapid march.
The next day, 4 May 1471, Edward IV deployed
his army for battle. He probably had around
4000 men; the Lancastrian force numbered
about 5000.

Edward IV followed much the same
deployment as he had used at Barnet. His
brother Gloucester commanded one flank battle
and William Hastings had the other. The centre
was commanded by Edward in person, aided by
his brother Clarence. Contemporary accounts
are somewhat confused about what order the
battles were deployed in; the usual practice was
to deploy from line of march with the vanguard
(Gloucester's command) taking the rightmost
position and the rearguard (Hastings) taking the
left. Some sources suggest that this order was
reversed, although they do not indicate a reason.

It is, however, generally agreed that Edward concealed a force of around 200 men in a wood on the left flank, either to prevent a Lancastrian flanking move through the wood or to mount a surprise attack if the opportunity arose. All of the Yorkist commanders were highly experienced and could be relied upon to give good account of themselves. With nothing more to do, Edward IV gave the order to attack.

Facing him was a Lancastrian position that benefited from some natural defensive features. A small watercourse protected part of the left flank, while the main battle was on higher ground. The going was tough as Edward's force advanced, with the rough terrain making it impossible to maintain both forward movement and any sort of battle order. As the Yorkist force struggled past ditches and embankments, Lancastrian artillery and archers kept up a steady fire. This was replied to in kind, and the Yorkist force turned out to be superior in both numbers of guns and the quality of their crews.

Somerset and Devon commanded the Lancastrian flank battles, with the centre nominally under the command of Edward of Westminster. John Wenlock, Baron Wenlock, was in actual command of the Lancastrian centre since Edward of Westminster had no experience. Wenlock had gone over to the Yorkist side after the first Battle of St Albans but had changed allegiance again to fight for the Lancastrian faction. There is no evidence of treachery on Wenlock's part, but he did fail to support Somerset's battle when it was most necessary, and so probably gave the day to the Yorkists. However, for a time it seemed that the Lancastrian defence would hold. Edward's advance ran into a surprise counter-attack led by Somerset, who had advanced using the rough terrain to conceal his force. With his battle strung out by the difficult advance, Edward was hard pressed but managed to repel this attack.

Below: Margaret of Anjou was taken prisoner after Tewkesbury, but was not treated harshly. She was eventually ransomed back to France and died in Anjou in 1482. She played no further role in the Wars of the Roses after the death of her son.

Edward was assisted by his brother Gloucester, who brought up elements of his battle, and by the force he had posted on the flank earlier. Attacked from the rear and heavily engaged to his front, Somerset's force collapsed and triggered a more widespread rout. Somerset managed to escape the chaos, seeking sanctuary in Tewkesbury Abbey though not before (according to legend) killing Baron Wenlock with an axe for failing to send timely support.

The Lancastrian force suffered heavy losses as it disintegrated. Rough terrain hemmed in men trying to flee. Some drowned in the river, some were trampled and some fought one another. Many more died in the pursuit at the hands of Yorkist soldiers. The Earl of Devon and Somerset's younger brother were killed on the field of battle, whilst Somerset and other Lancastrian leaders were brought from the abbey to face trial. Edmund Beaufort, Duke of Somerset, was summarily beheaded. With the

Above: According to some accounts, Edward of Westminster was violently slain by knights escorting King Edward IV, acting upon the king's orders. This version of events depicts him as maintaining his birthright to the throne to the very end.

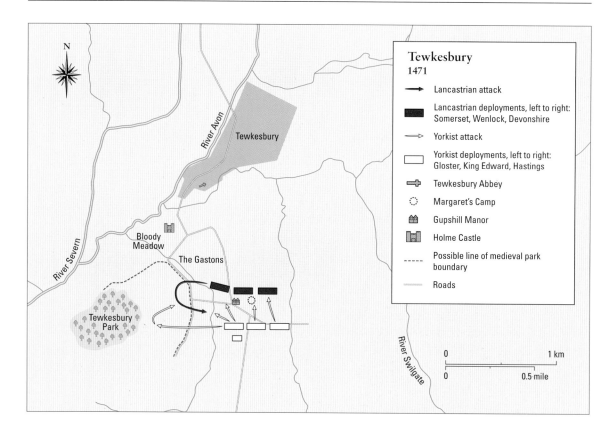

Above: It is difficult to discern a clear picture of the Battle of Tewkesbury from contemporary accounts. The difficult terrain played a key part in the events of the day, enabling concealed forces to attack by surprise.

death of his brother John in battle, this ended the male line of the Beauforts. Margaret of Anjou was captured soon after the battle – on 21 May – and imprisoned for the next five years.

Deaths of Henry VI and Edward of Westminster

Edward of Westminster, heir to the throne of Henry VI, was captured after the battle. According to some accounts he was put to death almost immediately by Clarence, who held a short mock trial and then beheaded the young prince. Other versions of the story have a defiant Edward of Westminster brought before Edward IV who demanded from him an explanation

for his invasion. The prince replied that he had come to regain his father's birthright. Edward IV is said to have then struck the prince in the face with his gauntlet, signalling the knights of his escort to cut the prisoner down. If this is true then the death of Edward of Westminster fell somewhere between combat, execution and murder. This ambiguity perhaps sums up the whole Wars of the Roses era.

Up until this point, Edward IV had been content to hold Henry VI as a prisoner, but after the Battle of Tewkesbury he decided to rid himself of the former king. Henry died by violence on 21 May 1471. It has been suggested that the killer was Gloucester, later to be crowned Richard III. Whether or not this is the case, Henry was a royal prisoner whose life was in the hands of his captors, and they answered to Edward IV. Ultimately, responsibility for the death of Henry rests with Edward even if he did

Above: According to the official version of events, Henry VI died shortly after the Battle of Tewkesbury of misery and sadness. It is far more likely that violence was the cause, probably instigated by Richard of Gloucester on the orders of Edward VI.

not directly order it – and it is very likely that he did. The official version of events was that Henry died of 'melancholy', and it was probably unsafe to challenge this assertion.

Peace did not immediately break out after Tewkesbury. There was some unrest in the north of the country, although it was not serious by the standards of the time. Pro-Lancastrian forces were still operating in Wales under the command of Jasper Tudor, a half-brother of Henry VI. Their mother, Catherine of Valois, had secretly married Owen Tudor despite objections from the great nobility after the death of her first husband King Henry V of England. Jasper Tudor had been Earl of Pembroke but was attainted after Edward IV

took the throne and was subsequently defeated in battle by William Herbert who was granted his titles. Jasper Tudor was recognized as Earl of Pembroke after the restoration of King Henry VI to the throne in 1470, but was captured at the Battle of Barnet and his title stripped again. He remained a staunch Lancastrian even then, and led a resistance for a time before escaping to the continent with Henry Tudor, to whom he acted as a tutor in military matters.

Meanwhile, a greater threat had emerged. Thomas Neville, an illegitimate son of William Neville, Earl of Kent, had landed at Sandwich with a large force. Thomas Neville was sometimes known as Thomas Fauconberg or 'the bastard of Fauconberg' for his father, who was a notable military commander. Thomas himself was a renowned leader and fighter, who had won fame fighting against pirates in the North Sea and the English Channel. He had been a Lancastrian but joined the Yorkist cause in 1460. After 1469, he sided with the Earl of Warwick and assisted him as a commander of naval forces. He had tried to stop Edward IV from reaching England but failed.

Thomas Neville raised an army in Kent whilst his ships moved to London. Refused entry, he attacked the city by dismounting cannon from his vessels to bombard the city's defences, then tried to storm the capital. This attack was repelled, though Thomas Neville was able to fall back with his army – reportedly 20,000 strong – still intact. Neville learned that Warwick was dead and his bid to depose Edward IV was over and he was ultimately captured at Southampton after his ships were taken at Sandwich by Edward's forces. He

was taken as a captive to Middleham Castle in Yorkshire and beheaded on 22 September 1471.

These events are often seen as ending the Wars of the Roses as such. A period of relative peace and stability began in England, ending with the death of Edward IV and a new conflict

---

'A period of relative peace and stability began in England, ending with the death of Edward IV and a new conflict over succession'.

---

over succession. However, that conflict had its origins in the Wars of the Roses and led to a final resurgence of the Yorkist–Lancastrian feud.

Stability Returns to England

From 1471 onwards, Edward IV had a solid position as king. There was still unrest, but he had sufficient power to suppress any rebellion and to restore stability to the country. His closest supporters were granted high offices, which sometimes caused friction. Edward's brother Richard of Gloucester was given large grants of land and appointed as a governor for the north of England. This gave him responsibility for defending the north from Scottish incursions, and perhaps not coincidentally took him away from court. He was kept busy dealing with raids and launching counter-raids, but this did not prevent him from getting into a serious dispute with his brother George, Duke of Clarence.

Left: Anne Neville, daughter of the Earl of Warwick, was betrothed to Edward of Westminster. After his death she married Richard of Gloucester. Her sister Isabel was already married to George of Clarence, Richard's brother, which created frictions over the division of the Warwick estate.

Gloucester married Anne Neville, younger sister to Isabel who was already married to his brother Clarence. This gave Gloucester a claim to parts of the large Neville inheritance, awarded in its entirety by his brother, and resulted in a lengthy dispute. Despite the intervention of their brother Edward, the two continued to feud for some time, although Gloucester did oppose Clarence's execution for treason. Clarence had already proven himself to be capable of great treachery. When his plan to marry Mary, Duchess of Burgundy, was blocked by Edward, Clarence removed himself from court and evidence emerged that he was plotting a rebellion. Tiring of his brother's intrigues, Edward had him arrested and charged with treason. He was attainted in January 1478 and executed in February. According to popular legend he was allowed to choose from a number of methods of execution and selected to be drowned in a butt of Malmsey wine.

In the interim, war with France briefly

Above: Allied with Charles of Burgundy, Edward IV began a campaign into France in 1475 but almost immediately accepted generous treaty terms offered by Louis XI of France. These included the payment of significant yearly sums and the ransom of Margaret of Anjou.

flared up. In alliance with Burgundy, Edward IV invaded France, but was quickly involved in peace negotiations. The subsequent Treaty of Pecquigny, signed in 1475, created a truce between England and France and an agreement to support one another against internal and external foes. Edward also received a large sum of cash. The treaty included an agreement that Edward's daughter, Elizabeth of York, would marry Charles, son of Louis XI of France. Margaret of Anjou was ransomed as part of the treaty. She retired to Anjou on a pension from Louis and played no further part in the conflict.

By 1480, Edward IV was primarily concerned with his own pleasure. Governance of the kingdom was largely in the hands of

ELIZABETH OF YORK

BORN IN 1466, Elizabeth of York was the eldest child of Edward IV and Elizabeth Woodville. Her father had been assured, by means of obscure astrological processes, that his child would be a boy. In fact Elizabeth was followed by two sisters before a male child was born. Elizabeth's godfather was Richard Neville, Earl of Warwick. Warwick would later become an enemy of the Woodvilles and of Edward IV, but for the time being he was a close friend of the family. During Elizabeth's childhood that changed dramatically, and her early life was lived in a period of great uncertainty. After 1471, stability had returned and Elizabeth's career as a royal princess was more assured. In 1475, as part of the Treaty of Pecquigny, Elizabeth was betrothed to Charles, heir to the throne of France. King Edward granted her part of the payment received from France at the Treaty of Pecquigny that agreed this marriage, making her independently wealthy.

As a result of the betrothal, Elizabeth's education was directed towards a future at the French court. She learned to read and write in French, and from 1480 onwards she was accorded all the honours appropriate to a future queen consort of France. That changed in 1483 when her father became ill. Correctly deducing that there was no longer any danger of an English invasion, Louis XI of France decided that the Treaty of Pecquigny no longer applied. He broke off the betrothal of his son to Elizabeth of York and began negotiations to marry him to Mary, Duchess of Burgundy.

With the death of Edward IV, the fortunes of the Woodville family plummeted. They had few friends, but had not needed many

Above: Elizabeth of York, daughter of Edward IV and Elizabeth Woodville, survived troubled times and changing circumstances to eventually marry Henry VII and thus found the Tudor dynasty. Their marriage was, by all accounts, happy as well as being politically important.

when they were the family of the king. Had Prince Edward been crowned as was his right, the Woodvilles might have remained at the forefront of English politics. Instead, he was imprisoned and met a mysterious death. Richard of Gloucester, brother to the late king, assumed the throne as Richard III.

Elizabeth of York and her family took

Left: As agreed between her mother and Henry Tudor, Elizabeth of York wed the new King Henry VII in 1486. Although troubles continued, this union of the houses of York and Lancaster effectively ended the Wars of the Roses as such.

During this uncomfortable time, Elizabeth's mother made an agreement with Henry Tudor that if he returned to England and took the throne, Elizabeth of York would marry him. Henry Tudor landed in August 1485, defeating Richard III in battle to claim the throne as Henry VII. He was crowned before his marriage to Elizabeth, but kept his promise to wed her once he had ensured that power was his alone. This marriage joined the houses of York and Lancaster and created a new dynasty, the Tudors.

Elizabeth had little political power or influence even after her marriage to the king, but she was well liked and was deeply mourned by her family when she died in 1503. Two of her five children did not survive to adulthood, but the three that did were destined for greatness. The surviving children of Henry VII and Elizabeth of York were Mary Tudor, who briefly became Queen of France, Margaret Tudor who married the King of Scotland and was grandmother to Mary, Queen of Scots, and Henry, who succeeded his father and reigned as Henry VIII.

refuge in Westminster Abbey, where they were granted sanctuary. After a time they surrendered themselves to the new king. Elizabeth of York was not treated unkindly, although her brothers were probably quietly murdered and she was declared illegitimate. This was due to a spurious claim that at the time of Edward IV's marriage to Elizabeth Woodville he was already betrothed to another lady, making his marriage invalid. This was not an attack on Elizabeth of York as such; she was just collateral damage in a bid to legitimize Richard III's coronation. With his older brother George executed for treason in 1478 and his brother, the king's children declared as bastards, his inheritance of the crown was legal under the normal rules of succession.

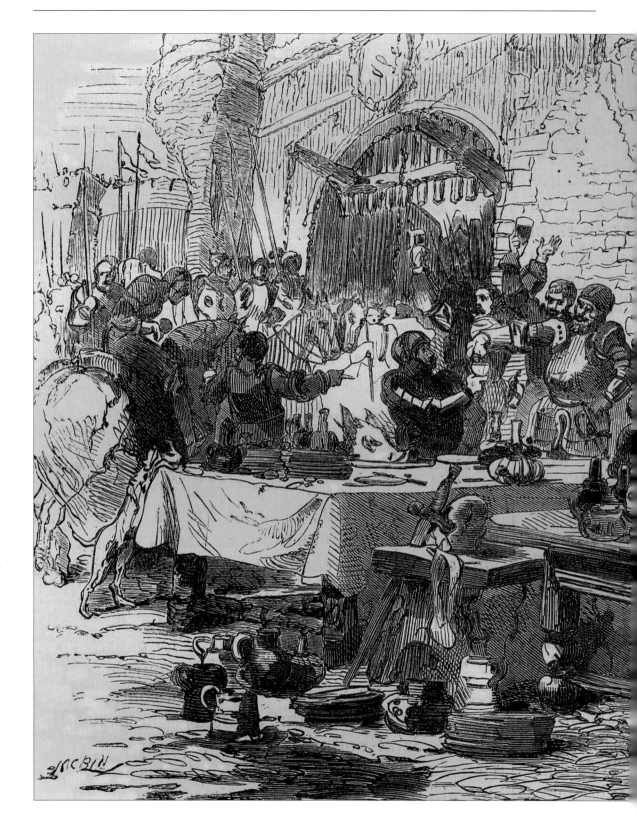

Left: The ability to provide a proper feast was one mark of a noble or a king's power. There were complex social rules for who sat where and served in what order. This feast was organized for the English Army after the Treaty of Pecquigny.

the Woodville family, whilst Edward's brother Gloucester held the north against the main remaining threat; Scotland. It fell to him to conduct the war that broke out as a result of French interference. Despite the fact that a seven-year truce was in place, France was seeking an alliance with Scotland against England. This resulted in a period of raiding and escalating tensions followed by open warfare in 1482. The town of Berwick changed hands twice, finally being retaken by Gloucester's forces and remaining an English possession thereafter.

'The relatively simple York/Lancaster divide had been blurred to the point where it was no longer as meaningful as previously'.

Gloucester was popular in the north of England, whilst his brother Edward retained his own popularity in the capital despite his excesses and general disaffection with the Woodville family. Despite wars with Scotland and France, and a possible plot on the part of Clarence, the years from 1471 to 1483 were relatively peaceful. Then, on 14 April 1483, King Edward IV of England died. The subsequent scramble for the throne of England was a coda to the Wars of the Roses proper. The relatively simple York/Lancaster divide had been blurred to the point where it was no longer as meaningful as previously, but the viciousness of the conflict that followed was undiminished.

RICHARD III

When Edward IV of England died on 9 April 1483, his eldest son
was too young to assume the throne. It was obvious that a Lord Protector
would have to be appointed, and the most suitable candidate was
the king's younger brother, Richard of Gloucester.

◆

'With Edward dead, Hastings' position was weakened.'

Richard of Gloucester had been the king's representative in the north of England for some years, and normally resided there. His main contact at court was William Hastings, a lifelong friend of King Edward and an opponent of the Woodville family, who dominated court affairs mainly due to the marriage of Elizabeth Woodville to the king. Hastings' own position was retained mainly due to his friendship with Edward, which

Richard III is one of the most controversial figures in English history and is better known from Shakespeare's portrayal than the reality of his life and reign. The death of Edward IV (above) created a period of instability as his heir was too young to rule.

overrode any political machinations of his wife's family. With Edward dead, Hastings' position was weakened although his good relations with Richard might be helpful.

King Edward seems to have been greatly saddened by the rift between his wife and his friend; not long before his death he asked them to make a reconciliation. However, Hastings remained suspicious of the Woodvilles, and when the queen proposed that the heir be escorted to London by a large force, Hastings vigorously opposed the idea. He stated that if the heir approached London with an army, he would remove himself to Calais where he was governor.

Edward, Prince of Wales, became King Edward V when his father died. Born in 1470 whilst his father was in exile, Edward was at the time of his father's death at Ludlow Castle, traditional residence of the Prince of Wales. He was under the protection of Anthony Woodville, Earl Rivers. Rivers was brother to the queen, and had served at times as admiral and in other important posts. He was assigned in 1471 as lieutenant of Calais but Hastings was then given the post instead, creating another bone of contention between the Woodvilles and Hastings.

Earl Rivers set out to escort his nephew to London for a hurried coronation organized by the boy's mother. She was engaged at the time in a power struggle with Hastings, who sought to prevent her from making new appointments for her family and favourites before Richard of Gloucester could take up the reins of power as Lord Protector as his dying brother had instructed. Hastings also informed Gloucester of these developments, urging him to come quickly to London. Although Edward V was only 12 years old and would not normally begin to rule until he reached his majority, there were precedents for younger kings to be crowned. Richard II was crowned when aged only 10, so it was possible that instead of a regency with Richard of Gloucester as Lord Protector the Woodville family might be able to control the country through their child king. This, however, depended on getting Edward to London and crowning him before anyone could interfere.

The Imprisonment of King Edward V

Richard of Gloucester managed to intercept Earl Rivers and the as-yet-uncrowned Edward *en route* for London. There was probably no reason for Rivers or Edward to suspect foul play, as Gloucester had always been loyal to Edward's father and had been nominated by him as Lord Protector of the realm until Edward came of age. Besides, Gloucester had authority on his side. To defy him was essentially an act of civil war, not something to be entered into without great certainty that he intended treachery. Unfortunately for Edward, that is

exactly what Richard of Gloucester intended. He dined with the King and his uncle, acting as if he were a friend, then had them arrested next morning. This was a grave breach of the laws of hospitality; a host was expected to protect his guests and even fight to defend them, yet Gloucester used the occasion to arrest and imprison Edward and his uncle.

> 'A host was expected to protect his guests and even fight to defend them, yet Gloucester used the occasion to arrest and imprison Edward and his Uncle'.

Earl Rivers and his son Sir Richard Grey were taken to Pontefract castle where they were held for a time. Richard Grey was a half-brother of Edward and was powerful in Wales. He was several years older than Edward V and had been something of a mentor to the boy. His lands and titles were given to others during his period of imprisonment, and on 25 June 1483 he and his father were executed on the orders of Richard of Gloucester, who was soon to ascend the throne as Richard III.

Upon hearing that her son had been captured, Elizabeth Woodville took her other children, including Richard, Duke of York, to the sanctuary at Westminster Abbey. This was a wise move, making it pointless to harm Edward whilst his younger brother Richard was safe.

Opposite: Having intercepted the young Edward, Prince of Wales, Richard of Gloucester escorted him to the capital. Since Richard was the appointed regent, little would seem amiss to those who did not know that Edward's original escort had been arrested and imprisoned.

Indeed, Elizabeth Woodville received a message from Hastings to the effect that if Richard of Gloucester tried to crown anyone other than Edward as king, Richard Duke of York would be crowned as a challenge. The implication was that Hastings and others were willing to fight to see the succession go ahead as determined by birthright.

This position is not surprising; Hastings was a lifelong friend of Edward IV, and probably saw any attempt to replace his son as king as treachery against Edward's memory. Thus

Opposite: Elizabeth Woodville agreed to allow her younger son Richard to join his brother Edward in the Tower of London. Until she did so, Edward's life was fairly safe as eliminating him would leave his brother as heir.

Above: Elizabeth Woodville was in a difficult situation even though she had been granted sanctuary. Her power had come from her husband and control of his heir. With one dead and the other imprisoned, she could not be certain of anyone's motives.

although he had been favourably disposed towards Richard of Gloucester, he now took the side of the Woodvilles even though he had always been their opponent. Again, this is not all that surprising; the Woodvilles were operating 'within the system' even though Hastings disapproved of them, whereas deposing the young Edward and seizing his crown was an entirely different matter.

The Woodville family remained in the sanctuary at Westminster, and the young Richard Duke of York with them, until Elizabeth

Left: Hastings made himself an obstacle to Richard's bid for the throne, so was quickly removed by arrest and execution. A major trial was probably undesirable; Richard wanted to seize power in as low-key manner as possible to avoid creating further opposition.

would befall the boys; preparations were ongoing for Edward's coronation. However, the boys met a mysterious fate at some point during their incarceration. They were widely assumed to have been murdered, although at whose orders remains unclear.

Richard's Bid for the Throne

Although Richard of Gloucester's plans to seize the throne were well advanced, preparations for the coronation of Edward, Prince of Wales as Edward V went on. The pretence of crowning Edward was presumably continued as a cover until Richard was ready to act, so the appointed date of 22 June was the moment when he must reveal his plan or change it.

In order to ensure his bid succeeded, Richard of Gloucester needed to remove his opponents from a position where they could interfere. To this end, on 13 or 14 June, Gloucester called a council at which he denounced Elizabeth Woodville and Jane Shore,

Woodville was persuaded to allow Richard to be taken to the Tower. The ostensible reason was that his brother Edward was unhappy, having no-one to play with, and the presence of his brother would be a great comfort to him. At the time there was no reason to assume that harm

who had been a mistress of both Edward IV and Hastings. The women were accused of sorcery, which Gloucester allegedly 'proved' by showing the council his withered arm. Hastings was accused of treason, arrested and summarily beheaded. Lord Stanley and John Morton, Archbishop of Canterbury, were also arrested. Lord Stanley was injured during the arrest by one of Gloucester's men who took a swipe at him for unknown reasons. Stanley was not imprisoned for long, although he had been a champion of the imprisoned Edward V, and was instead granted high office by Gloucester.

After this, Richard of Gloucester more or less controlled the situation in London.

On 22 June, the expected day of Edward's coronation, it was announced that the children of Edward IV and Elizabeth Woodville were illegitimate. The somewhat thin pretext for this was that Edward IV had previously intended to marry Eleanor Talbot before meeting Elizabeth Woodville, and thus their marriage was declared invalid. This made their children bastards and thus they were ineligible to inherit the throne.

Below: Richard of Gloucester created circumstances under which it was logical – to outward appearances at least – that he should be offered the crown. He made a token show of reluctance which failed to convince many of those present.

THE PRINCES IN THE TOWER

SOON AFTER THE death of Edward IV, his son Edward, Prince of Wales was summoned to London to be crowned. Intercepted by Richard of Gloucester, Edward was instead taken to the Tower of London and imprisoned. There was for a time a polite fiction that Edward was being protected whilst preparations were made for his coronation, although it is not clear how widely this was accepted. Edward's brother Richard, Duke of York, who was nine years old at the

time, was brought to join him soon afterward. Richard had taken refuge in Westminster Abbey with his mother and sisters, but was persuaded to surrender himself into the protection of Richard of Gloucester, Lord Protector of the realm and the boys' uncle. Richard was to be a companion for his brother, who was said to be lonely in his confinement.

At some point after Richard of Gloucester was crowned as Richard III of England, the boys disappeared. The discovery of two skeletons by workmen in 1674 lends credence to the idea that they were quietly murdered and buried in the grounds of the Tower of London, although there is no clear evidence that this occurred. It was claimed, and it is still believed today by some, that one or both of the boys escaped their captivity. According to Sir Thomas More, the princes were murdered on the orders of Richard III, presumably to remove any opposition to his rule that might coalesce around them. Moore states that the Constable of the Tower, Sir Robert Brackenbury, was ordered to put the boys to death and refused, but was unable to decline an order to hand over keys to Sir James Tyrell. Tyrell was a close supporter of Richard III, who had fought alongside him in Scotland and won distinction. Tyrell was elevated to high office by Richard III, but that does not necessarily equate to a reward for being the agent of royal murder. Some have suggested that Tyrell did away with the princes

Left: The story of the 'princes in the tower' is used by many to blacken the villain of their choice. Whatever happened to the boys, they were victims of the reality of the times – high station brought with it grave risks even for the innocent.

later, on the orders of Henry VII. He did serve Henry VII in high offices, although later he was imprisoned in the Tower for treachery and beheaded. Tyrell confessed to the murder of the princes before his execution.

If Thomas More's account is correct, then some time in late 1483 Tyrell gave access to the boys' accommodation to the men sent to murder them. They were smothered with pillows, an easy thing to accomplish against a child, and afterward their bodies were secretly buried. This account is generally accepted, although there is no proof to be had. Indeed, the possibility exists that the boys were not killed at all. It is possible that one or both of the princes died of natural causes, which was not uncommon in the period, or that claims that they escaped are in fact true. Two pretenders to the throne claimed to be Richard, Duke of York, and based their claims on the story of an escape from captivity. At least one of these stories must be untrue, but there was some support for the claims among those who knew the princes.

On balance, it seems likely that the boys were indeed killed whilst in the Tower of London. However, exactly who ordered the murders is an open question. Richard III probably had the most to gain from the deed, but it may have been one of his subordinates acting alone, or Henry VII. Henry did execute a number of potential threats upon taking the throne, so it is possible that he had the princes taken out of the equation to ensure there were no threats to his reign. Given the turbulence of the past decades that would seem like a prudent move, but again there is no proof one way or the other.

With Edward, Prince of Wales' claim (and that of his younger brother Richard of York) thus put aside, next in line to the throne was of course Edward IV's surviving brother, Richard of Gloucester. He was crowned King Richard III of England on 6 July, and began a royal progress soon afterward. Having succeeded in making himself king, Richard now needed to secure his position and deal with any challenges that might appear.

Buckingham's Rebellion

Henry Stafford, Duke of Buckingham, is generally credited with leading the uprising against Richard III that occurred in late 1483. He was an extremely powerful and important man, descended through his mother from John of Gaunt, and was married to Catherine Woodville who was sister to the queen. Buckingham's father and grandfather had both been killed in battle fighting for the House of Lancaster, but the York/Lancaster divide was becoming less relevant as a new political reality emerged. He assisted Richard of Gloucester in capturing Edward, Prince of Wales, and was well rewarded with several high offices. Thus his loyalty to Richard III should have been considerable. It certainly seemed so on 24 June 1483 when he made an eloquent speech in favour of crowning Richard as king.

Buckingham seems to have become disaffected with Richard's reign quite quickly, and left court in August 1483. It is possible that he was influenced by John Morton, Archbishop of Canterbury. The latter had

Below: The rebellion of Henry, Duke of Buckingham, was one of several revolts that arose from the turbulent Wars of the Roses era but which were not part of the York/Lancaster conflict as such. By 1483 the former factions were increasingly irrelevant.

been arrested at the same time as Hastings, and was placed under Buckingham's supervision. Yet during this period Buckingham turned against Richard and entered into correspondence with Elizabeth Woodville. He also conspired with Henry Tudor, who was at that time preparing to land in England with his followers.

Buckingham planned to lead an uprising that would coincide with the arrival of Henry Tudor, but from the start

'The rebellion collapsed and Buckingham's army disintegrated. He attempted to flee but was betrayed and subsequently executed'.

his plans went awry. Henry Tudor's fleet was unable to cross the Channel due to storms, and Buckingham's army was prevented from crossing the Severn into England by a flood. The rebellion collapsed and Buckingham's army disintegrated. He attempted to flee but was betrayed and subsequently executed on 2 November 1483.

Henry Tudor Lands in England

Henry Tudor was born in 1457. He never met his father, who was killed a few months before Henry's birth, and he suffered a troubled childhood. Henry was protected as well as possible by being moved from one castle to another in Wales, but much of the time these castles were under siege. His uncle, Jasper Tudor, did his best to protect the young Henry and ultimately became his tutor in military matters.

Henry Tudor was the son of Edmund of Hadham, whose father Owen Tudor married Catherine Valois who was the widow of Henry V. His father was half-brother to Henry VI, but was far more closely related to the French throne than the English. Indeed, Henry

Above: Buckingham's revolt was undone largely by water. His army was unable to cross the swollen river Severn, whilst forces coming across the Channel were forced back into port by storms. The rebellion then collapsed without striking a blow.

Tudor's blood claim to the throne of England was somewhat tenuous even without legal complications. His claim was based upon descent from Edward III, by way of John of Gaunt and his third wife Katherine Swynford. The two had several children before they were married, who were legitimized by the marriage but were legally barred from succession. Opponents stated that this made Henry Tudor's claim invalid; supporters decided that it did not matter.

It is probable that the Yorkist faction also thought that Henry Tudor's blood claim was so weak that it did not matter. They made no special attempt to eliminate him, even when at the age of four he was captured at the fall of Pembroke Castle. He received his education whilst in captivity and was not ill-treated. He remained a prisoner until the restoration of Henry VI to the throne, and was then brought to court by his uncle Jasper Tudor. The return of Edward IV forced both to flee to Brittany.

Despite being a distant relative with legal irregularities about his claim, by 1483 Henry Tudor was the best remaining Lancastrian candidate, since so many heirs had been slain in battle or executed over the preceding decades. The unstable political situation caused by Richard III's seizure of the throne created an opportunity that could be exploited. The first attempt, launched in 1483 with the support of Francis II, Duke of Brittany, failed when rough seas forced Henry's fleet back into port.

The total collapse of the rebellion led by the Duke of Buckingham deprived Henry Tudor of ready-made support in England, and set back his plans considerably. He did, however, have the support of the Woodville family and an agreement that if he were successful in taking the crown of England

Left: Henry Tudor chose to land in Wales, where he could expect to find at least some popular support and whose country he knew. The area was less likely to be firmly under royal control than much of England.

Elizabeth of York would marry him. This would legitimize his claim to the throne beyond any doubt and hopefully cement the support of many nobles. As previous events had shown, it was one thing to seize the throne and another to keep it.

'Henry Tudor was continually receiving reinforcements, albeit in small numbers, as disaffected nobles and their personal forces joined the Lancastrian host'.

Richard III tried to forestall Henry Tudor's plans by coercing Duke Francis to hand him over. Henry and his close supporters prudently moved to France, where they received extensive support. This enabled Henry to raise a modest army, mostly of French and Scottish troops, and to land them at Milford Haven in Wales on 7 August 1485. Upon his arrival, Henry Tudor was joined by a significant force of Welshmen, and many English nobles who had become disaffected with Richard III's reign also joined his cause either before or after he left France. This gave him a chance to defeat Richard III in open battle, but only if he acted quickly. Henry Tudor's entire force was in play, whereas Richard had reinforcements that could be called up from other regions, and was able to raise more troops if the campaign went on for any length of time.

Henry Tudor marched to Shrewsbury and then to Tamworth, arriving on 18 August. On the 20th he moved to Atherstone, whilst the Royal army under Richard III camped at Bosworth on the 21st. The following day the two armies clashed between Bosworth and Atherstone.

The Battle of Bosworth

Richard III commanded a force that somewhat outnumbered his enemies, but he had cause for misgivings. Henry Tudor was continually receiving reinforcements, albeit in small numbers, as disaffected nobles and their personal forces joined the Lancastrian host. Although Richard had reinforcements available, they would take time to arrive, and he could not be sure that his army would retain its fighting spirit for long. He thus needed to win a decisive battle as soon as possible.

Richard drew up his army in the usual three battles. He commanded the centre, with the left under Henry Percy, Earl of Northumberland and the right under John Howard, Duke of

Below: The confrontation at Bosworth Field began in an atmosphere of paranoia and treachery. Richard III could not be sure who would fight even among his loyal supporters, whereas Henry Tudor at least knew who was on his side and who was not.

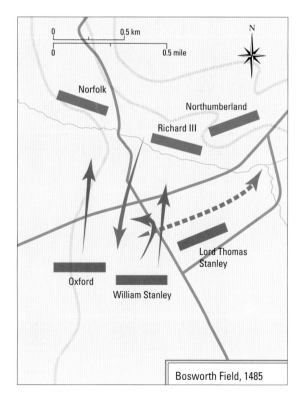

Bosworth Field, 1485

Above: The two armies drew close on the eve of the battle, but did not immediately engage. Medieval strategists preferred to wait for daybreak and fight a decisive action rather than chance everything on a wild scramble in darkness.

Norfolk. An additional force under Thomas, Lord Stanley, was nearby but Richard could not be sure of its intentions. He suspected Stanley of treachery (rightly so, in this case) and was holding his son hostage for his good behaviour. Stanley had already been arrested once, at the Tower of London along with Hastings, but was released and given great responsibilities. That trust turned out to be misplaced; Lord Stanley and his brother Sir William Stanley had reached an accommodation with Henry, although they would not openly join his forces at that point. Thus neither commander could be certain what the Stanleys would do, but both had reason to believe that they might come to his assistance once battle was joined.

Knowing that he lacked the experience to take on Richard III, Henry Tudor decided to take command of the reserve instead of leading the battle. His force was deployed with his infantry in the centre commanded by John de

Vere, Earl of Oxford, and cavalry on the flanks. Oxford, recognizing that he was outnumbered, ordered his troops to stay within ten paces of their standards. This ensured that his force would not become strung out and would present a dense mass to the enemy.

Both forces fielded a body of bowmen pushed forward to harass the enemy and the battle opened, as was usual, with an exchange of archery and an ineffective cannonade. Henry Tudor elected to attack despite being outnumbered. His force struggled through the marsh in front of the enemy positions and was fired upon by Richard's artillery. Richard, meanwhile, sent an order to Lord Stanley to join his force immediately, following it with an instruction to execute Stanley's son when he did not obey. This command was also not obeyed, with the executioners perhaps prudently waiting to see who won the battle before becoming responsible for the death of a potentially victorious nobleman's son. Meanwhile, Norfolk's battle engaged the Tudor army, although some of his troops seemed highly reluctant to join the fighting. This prompted Oxford to advance more boldly and brought about a fierce hand-to-hand struggle.

Below: With his army disintegrating or refusing to enter combat – or possibly about to betray him – Richard III staked everything on a drive straight at Henry Tudor. His bold charge brought him close to his enemy, but was ultimately unsuccessful.

Richard III sent reinforcements to Norfolk, but even with this assistance the royal army could make little headway. Norfolk himself was killed and his battle pushed back. Still Northumberland did not join the fighting, although he was ordered to do so by Richard. He stated that his force needed to remain in position to counter any move by the Stanleys. Whether or not that was true, it took a third of the royal army out of the equation.

In and of itself this might not have ensured Richard III's defeat, but he already suspected treachery from the Stanleys; he was quite prepared to believe that Northumberland had betrayed him too. There did remain a chance to win the day, however. Henry Tudor's escort was moving towards the Stanleys' position and might be out of reach of assistance. Richard led his personal retinue of about eighty knights in a charge at Henry's escort, hoping to kill him and win a decisive victory. Richard's attack was vigorous and initially successful; according to some accounts he personally killed Henry Tudor's standard-bearer and engaged Henry

Below: A rather romanticized depiction of the death of Richard III. His body was subsequently mutilated after his armour had been stripped off, and was then taken to Leicester. It was buried in Greyfriars church rather than in a royal tomb.

Right: According to many versions of the story, Richard III's crown was taken and stashed in a hawthorn bush by a looter, but was subsequently found and given to Henry Tudor. Henry was then hailed as King Henry VII by his victorious army.

directly for a time. However, Lord Stanley now joined the fight on the side of Henry Tudor, whilst Richard's retinue became surrounded.

Although aware that the day was lost, or perhaps because he knew it was, Richard III refused to flee the field. Some accounts have him turning away those who tried to bring him a horse to escape upon, and stating that he intended to die as the King of England. This may have been incredible stubbornness, raw courage, heroic despair at being completely betrayed or the realization that to flee was to be humiliated and executed at some point in the future, but for whatever reason Richard III stood his ground and fought until he was killed.

> 'Accounts have him turning away those who tried to bring him a horse to escape upon, and stating that he intended to die as the King of England'.

The royal army disintegrated and was pursued, but without any real enthusiasm. Richard's crown was found and given to Henry Tudor, who was proclaimed King of England by right of conquest. Henry Percy was arrested but was soon released and elevated to high office, whilst Lord Stanley was granted the Earldom of Derby for his service.

Henry VII

Henry Tudor was crowned Henry VII of England on 30 October 1485, and married Elizabeth of York as he had promised on 18 January 1486. This created the Tudor dynasty, whose symbol was a red and white rose, and essentially ended the Wars of the Roses. In truth, the traditional divisions between the Houses

of York and Lancaster had become much less meaningful. Although Henry was a Lancastrian and Richard III a Yorkist, many of those who rallied to Henry's banner when he landed in England were Yorkists.

Henry VII took a number of political and legal steps to cement his control over the country. He repealed the declaration that Edward IV's marriage was invalid, which made his wife Elizabeth of York once again a legitimate child of the king and queen. This made concrete the claim to the throne asserted by his children with Elizabeth and forestalled any further disputes about whose claim was more solid. Henry also declared that his reign began on 21 August 1485. This meant that anyone who had taken the field against him at Bosworth the next day was a traitor whose lands and titles could be stripped and passed to Henry's supporters. This measure was used sparingly, however; Henry forgave many who had raised arms against him and declared soon after his coronation that anyone who would swear fealty to him would not suffer for their part in the recent conflict.

There were those who were not forgiven, however. Among them was the son of George, Duke of Clarence. Although only ten years old the boy, Edward, Earl of Warwick, was a potential threat if a plot developed around him. He was imprisoned in the Tower of London from 1485 until 1499, when he was put on trial for treason. It was alleged that Warwick had been conspiring from within the Tower. He pleaded guilty and was beheaded, ending the male Plantagenet line.

Despite these measures, and laws passed by Henry VII to reduce the ability of great nobles to raise private armies, his reign was challenged by rebellions on several occasions. The first, led by Viscount Lovell and the brothers Humphrey and Thomas Stafford, was a shambles. Viscount Lovell attempted to raise a rebellion 1486 but apparently lost his nerve and instead fled to

Above: A stained-glass depiction of Tudor notables including Henry Tudor (Henry VII) and Jasper Tudor. The latter was restored to his title as Earl of Pembroke and elevated to the rank of Duke of Bedford for his unwavering support of Henry.

Burgundy. The Stafford brothers did cause some unrest but this collapsed almost immediately. The Staffords took advantage of the custom of granting sanctuary in order to escape justice by taking shelter in Tewkesbury Abbey, but were forcibly arrested anyway. This drew protests from the Pope, in turn leading to an agreement whereby sanctuary did not apply to traitors against the crown.

The next major challenge occurred in 1487, when one Lambert Simnel claimed to be the imprisoned Edward Earl of Warwick. Members of the Irish nobility supported him, along with Viscount Lovell and John de la Pole, Earl of Lincoln. The imposter was crowned as Edward VI in Ireland and landed in England with an army of German mercenaries. Henry VII personally led his army against the rebels, whose mercenary contingent was very skilled but outnumbered. The resulting Battle of Stoke is generally considered to be the last action of the Wars of the Roses, although arguably that period was now over and the rebellions were more about opposition to a new Tudor dynasty. The rebels were crushed and Lambert Simnel was taken prisoner. However, rather than being put to death as was common for traitors against the crown he was instead put to work – Henry VII gave him a job in the royal kitchens, as he was obviously just a figurehead.

From 1490, another imposter by the name of Perkin Warbeck began to make a nuisance of himself. Warbeck was convinced by Henry VII's opponents to impersonate Richard, Duke of York. The latter was assumed to have been

RICHARD III

BORN IN OCTOBER 1452, the youngest son of Richard Plantagenet, Duke of York, Richard of Gloucester remains a controversial figure in English history. He has been much maligned over the years, not least in Shakespeare's play. The latter is not too surprising. Shakespeare was writing in an England ruled by the Tudors, and Richard III was the king they deposed to take the throne. Shakespeare's *Richard III* is better known than the real history of the time, and this can colour the perceptions of even serious historians.

Richard III was a great nobleman of his times. He may or may not have ordered the murder of the 'Princes in the Tower', but he certainly put others to death in cold blood. To the modern observer his actions may seem cruel or downright evil, but they were no different to those of other monarchs. Richard of Gloucester, later Richard III, was living in an era of treachery and violence, and took measures to ensure his own survival as well as furthering his own ambitions. This does not make him any different from other monarchs who carried out much the same actions, for the same reasons, in the same era.

The question of Richard III's deformity has puzzled historians for many years. He is often portrayed as a twisted hunchback, and is recorded as having a withered arm. At one point he claimed that this was the result of evil sorcery practiced against him by his enemies, but it was more likely the result of a twisted spine. Far from

Left: Richard III (played here by Laurence Olivier) is most commonly associated with the hunchbacked villain created by Shakespeare. The Bard was of course producing his plays in an era dominated by those who overthrew Richard. He was thus unlikely to receive sympathetic treatment in the fiction of the day.

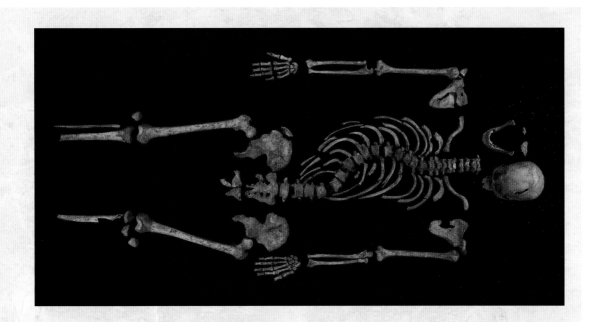

being a lurching hunchback, Richard III was able to wield a two-handed pollaxe in full armour. He fought in several battles and was skilled enough to overcome other warriors who presumably did not suffer any deformity of the spine. Thus any physical imperfection he had did not prevent him from being a formidable warrior. Proponents of Richard III have long claimed that his deformity was pure invention. The truth, as it so often does, falls between the two versions. Discovery of Richard III's body in 2012 and study of his skeleton indicated that he suffered from a quite severe curvature of the spine, but there was no evidence of a withered arm. The body did have severe injuries, some of them clearly post-mortem. Richard III probably died from a head wound inflicted by a heavy cutting weapon, with other injuries inflicted as a form of humiliation after he was dead. Some could only have been received after his armour was removed, which would not be possible while he was alive and fighting back. After his body had been mutilated in this fashion Richard III

Above: Discovery of Richard III's body finally resolved the question of his 'hunched back'. He did indeed suffer from a curvature of the spine, but was nevertheless a physically adept individual capable of fighting effectively in full armour.

was carried from the battlefield over the back of a horse and buried in a shallow grave at Greyfriars Church in Leicester, England.

It remained there until recently rediscovered. DNA tests on the skeleton have revealed there may be a genetic anomaly which could mean there is a break in the male line. This leads to questions about whether some monarchs such as Henry VI, Henry VII and Henry VIII had royal blood, and therefore the right to rule. Opinions about his life remain divided. He was a ruthless man but he was probably no different to any other nobleman of the time, just more powerful than most. And, his reputation has been blackened by one of the most influential writers of all time. Richard III's greatest crime, if it can be considered such, was that he was not on the side that got to write the history books.

Right: The Wars of the Roses flared up one last time when Lambert Simnel, posing as the last of the Plantagenets, raised an army against Henry VII. The rebel army, strengthened by foreign mercenaries, was nevertheless defeated by Henry VII.

murdered in the Tower of London, but there were those that insisted that he had escaped and Warbeck played on this belief with some success. He received support from several exiled nobles or foreign powers that opposed Henry VII's reign, notably Margaret, Duchess of Burgundy. France and Scotland also supported him, although whether or not they actually believed he was who he claimed is an open question – possibly they just wanted to stir up trouble for the English monarchy as part of the endless schemes that characterized politics in the era.

> 'Perkin Warbeck made several forays into England in the hope of stirring up rebellion, although without much success'.

Perkin Warbeck made several forays into England in the hope of stirring up rebellion, although without much success. His 1497 visit to Scotland encouraged the Scots to launch an attack into England, and in order to pay for the conflict Henry VII levied taxes. This in turn caused the people of Cornwall to revolt in protest. Warbeck joined the rebels who marched on London. They were around 16,000 strong when they were joined by James Touchet, Baron Audley. Audley took command, as he was the only man among the rebels who had any idea how to lead a fighting force. The rebels were confronted by a royal army at Blackheath, London where they were completely out-generalled. With no cavalry or artillery, the rebels were flanked and attacked

Opposite: Henry VII's mercy towards Lambert Simnel might
have been a clever way of showing the world that he really
was an imposter. No great nobleman would take a job in the
kitchens; Simnel's acceptance confirmed that he was not
Edward, Earl of Warwick.

from the rear as well as the front, but still put
up a stubborn fight. Afterward, Audley and
some of the rebel leaders were found guilty
of treason. Due to his rank, Audley was lucky
enough to be beheaded whilst the commoners
were hanged, drawn and quartered. The vast
majority of the rebels were pardoned, but
Perkin Warbeck was not. He had deserted his
followers before the Battle of Blackheath, but
later surrendered. He was later charged with
conspiring with the imprisoned Edward, Earl
of Warwick and was hanged in 1499.

Henry VII's rule was not seriously challenged
by these rebellions, and having reduced the
private forces the nobility could wield, he
secured his power by weakening theirs. He also
implemented more effective taxation and control
over the finances of the kingdom, ushering in
an era of if not prosperity, then at least fiscal
stability. His marriage to Elizabeth of York was
apparently happy, although marred by the death
of their first son Arthur in 1502.

The death of Elizabeth of York in 1503
affected Henry VII badly, and although he
made some vague efforts in the direction of
another marriage, his heart was not in it. He
died in 1509, leaving a very much changed
England. The dynastic feuding of the past 50
years was finally over, and as Henry VII's son
Henry was crowned Henry VIII of England, he
assumed control of a much stronger and more
stable realm than any English King had for
many years.

Below: Perkin Warbeck was closely watched after his capture,
but not punished. When he tried to flee he was recaptured and
pilloried, then subsequently charged with further conspiracy
and put to death by hanging in November 1499.

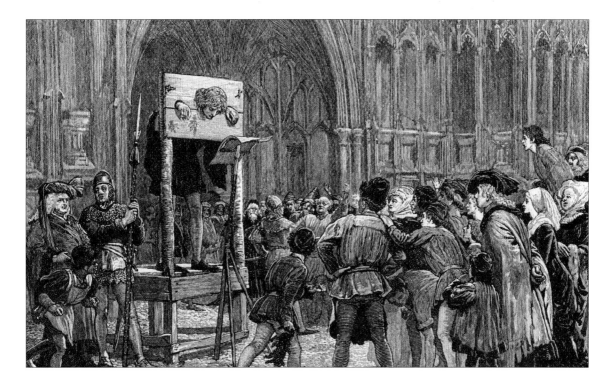

THE LEGACY OF THE WARS OF THE ROSES

The Renaissance is often considered to have begun in England at the end of the Wars of the Roses. This is more of a convenient date than any indication of instant change in society of course, but the return of stability to England did permit Renaissance ideas to take hold and begin to flower.

———◆———

'It was Henry VIII who dictated how England would respond'.

The battles of the Wars of the Roses can be considered to be the last truly medieval clashes; new technology began to be far more prevalent and the nature of warfare underwent major changes in the next century.

Stability had political effects too. As well as the obvious ability of a powerful English nation to intervene in affairs elsewhere,

Henry VII introduced Renaissance thinkers such as Erasmus and Thomas More to his children at court in Greenwich. More would later serve Henry VIII (above) as a key advisor, and finally be executed on his order.

the end of a turbulent time also removed opportunities for foreign powers to become involved in adventures in England. This meant that instead of supporting one faction or another in England, hoping to gain some long-term advantage, the attention of European monarchs was directed elsewhere. It is not always possible to see the results of a negative event of this sort, but the absence of English internal conflicts to become involved in had consequences for the policies of other countries and therefore the targets to which they turned their attention.

Henry VIII

Henry VIII, second son of Henry VII of England, reigned from 1509 to 1547. This

Left: Henry VIII's desire for a male heir was not simply vanity; he knew what could befall his realm if there was no clear line of succession. This in turn drove him to seek a wife who could provide strong sons.

generally remembered as a very physical man. However, he was also a scholar and a talented musician, with many books and musical instruments. In this, he was very much a Renaissance man although the Renaissance was slower to spread to England outside the royal court. Henry also liked luxury to the point of excess, and spent vast sums on lavish spectacles such as tourneys that rapidly demolished the royal budget. His overseas wars were another drain on the coffers.

Henry VIII may or may not have taken a warning from the fate of his weak and pliable predecessor Henry VI, but certainly he was the exact opposite. He took the idea that a king needed to be strong-willed to a whole new level, espousing the concept of a divine right of kings – basically that his authority came straight from God. To signify this divine backing he was the first English monarch to use the phrase 'by the grace of God' in his title.

Whilst there was undoubtedly an element of ego about Henry VIII's desire for a male heir, he would have been mindful of the consequences of a disputed succession and keen to prevent it. Had his succession of wives merely been about desire or love, he might well have maintained them as mistresses. This was not uncommon; several women had risen to prominence as mistresses of the monarch or his close associates. Henry wanted more than liaisons with women he desired – he wanted a wife who could bear him legitimate sons.

Henry's quest for a male heir resulted in six marriages and a series of shenanigans every time he decided to rid himself of one. Since

was a time of great change; indeed Henry VIII caused some of those changes. Others would have happened anyway, but it was Henry VIII who dictated how England would respond and therefore what effects those changes might have.

Henry was not expected to inherit the throne, but the death of his elder brother Arthur in 1502 made him heir apparent. He was not properly educated in kingship and governance when he ascended the throne, but he had learned some lessons from recent history. Among them was the need for a clear succession, and this would be a driving force in events that changed the world. As a young man Henry was warlike and athletic. He enjoyed sports, including jousting and real tennis, and is

he could not divorce his wives, Henry VIII had to dispose of them in other ways if they displeased him by failing to produce an heir. One of Henry's wives died of natural causes, one outlived him. Of the four he rid himself of, two were beheaded and two marriages were annulled for fairly spurious reasons.

This brought Henry into conflict with the Pope, who would not give him what he wanted by legitimizing the annulment of his first marriage to Catherine of Aragon. Another man might have stopped short of challenging this, at the time the most potent authority on Earth, but Henry decided to break with the Catholic Church. This ultimately led to the Reformation and the creation of the Church of England, and many years of conflict between Catholics and Protestants in England. In the interim, Henry's dissolution of the monasteries brought in vast riches for the crown in the short term and created massive changes in the nature of English religion.

PARVVLE PATRISSA, PATRIÆ VIRTVTIS ET HÆRES
ESTO, NIHIL MAIVS MAXIMVS ORBIS HABET.
GNATVM VIX POSSVNT COELVM ET NATVRA DEDISSE,
HVIVS QVEM PATRIS, VICTVS HONORET HONOS.
ÆQVATO TANTVM, TANTI TV FACTA PARENTIS,
VOTA HOMINVM, VIX QVO PROGREDIANTVR, HABENT
VINCITO, VICISTI, QVOT REGES PRISCVS ADORAT
ORBIS, NEC TE QVI VINCERE POSSIT, ERIT.

After Henry VIII

At the time of his death in 1547, Henry VIII had no adult male heir. His son Edward, born to Jane Seymour, was nine years old and could not rule in his own right. England once again had a Lord Protector, initially in the person of Edward Seymour, Earl of Hertford. Edward VI was crowned on 20 February 1547, with actual power wielded by a regency council headed by the Lord Protector.

Edward VI's reign was troubled, with unrest and financial problems piling on top of a war with Scotland. However, there was no repeat of the dynastic squabbling that took place during the Wars of the Roses until

Left: Henry VIII had only one son. He was crowned Edward VI at the age of nine and did not live long enough to reach majority. He nominated Lady Jane Grey as his successor, although her reign was extremely short.

Edward was discovered to be terminally ill. Aged just 15, Edward VI died and was succeeded – briefly – by Lady Jane Grey. Grey was Edward's cousin; his half-sisters Mary and Elizabeth were closer to the throne but were barred from the succession. Lady Jane Grey ruled for less than two weeks before being deposed in favour of Edward V's half-sister Mary. Mary was the daughter of Henry VIII and his first wife Catherine of Aragon and had been excluded from succession because she was a Catholic.

Above: Lady Jane Grey was deposed in favour of Henry VIII's daughter Mary, and in the process was convicted of treason. Initially spared, she was executed on the order of Queen Mary in 1554; essentially an innocent victim of politics.

Under Mary's rule, measures were taken to reverse the Reformation and curb Protestantism in England with sufficient zeal that she became known as Bloody Mary. This policy was reversed after Mary's death in 1558, at which point her half-sister Elizabeth took the throne. Elizabeth was the child of Henry VIII and his second wife, Anne Boleyn. She had been declared illegitimate when her mother's marriage to the king was annulled, and had spent some time imprisoned on suspicion of supporting English Protestants against the counter-reforms of Mary.

Elizabeth reigned as Elizabeth I from 1553 to 1603. She worked to settle the complex religious questions besetting England, and created the basis for the modern Church of England. It was during her reign that the Renaissance truly flowered in England and the Middle Ages were left behind, and for this reason the term 'Elizabethan' has a similar meaning in England to 'Renaissance' in a wider context when referring to a cultural and social era.

Although Elizabeth I did not become greatly involved in overseas wars, she did support Protestant rebels against Spanish rule in the Low Countries. English privateers also preyed upon Spanish treasure ships returning from the New World, which did nothing to endear England to the King of Spain. Eventually, war came and in 1588 Philip II of Spain sent a great armada to carry his invasion force to England. This was defeated by the English navy, although the English Armada sent out in 1589 to attack Spanish shipping performed rather badly. Nevertheless, Elizabeth I proved to be a strong leader who provided stability and social progress. She weathered her troubles with overall success, although by the time of her death in 1603 she had serious financial difficulties and there was significant unrest in the country. Elizabeth never married, and thus had no heirs to inherit her throne.

Opposite: Elizabeth I provided strong and generally successful leadership during her reign, but left behind no heirs. With her death in 1603 the Tudor dynasty came to an end, but its legacy was a far stronger and more stable realm.

Elizabeth I died in 1603, and with her ended the Tudor dynasty. The throne of England passed to James VI of Scotland, who was crowned as James I of England. This was not without contention, but again there was no civil war as there had been during the Wars of the Roses. The Tudor dynasty had emerged from that chaos and was successful in restoring a measure of greatly needed stability to England; sufficiently so that this new stability outlasted the family that created it.

The Tudors also were responsible for the creation of a powerful navy that would be the instrument and hallmark of British power for centuries to come, and the Church of England, which created a strong Protestant nation at a time of great religious turbulence. The Wars of Religion which wracked Europe from around 1560 might have taken a different course if England had remained a Catholic country. The affairs of the New World might also have proceeded differently without an England in possession of a powerful navy and in opposition to Spain. The same navy was instrumental in carving out and protecting the British Empire. These later events were greatly influenced by the actions of the Tudor dynasty, and those in turn originated from the Wars of the Roses.

Beyond a certain point, it is not possible

Below: The defeat of the Spanish Armada in 1588 established England as a major naval power. This had huge implications for world history, notably in the settlement of the Americas and the rush for colonial possessions that followed.

as they were (so far as can be ascertained) and events taking place at the times and places, and in the manner, that they historically did.

It is possible to take a few liberties with history and still create a basically accurate story. Thus some authors have extrapolated complex tales from what little is known about the historical events, retaining plausibility by ensuring that where an event is recorded, the fictional story ties in with it. Filling in the blanks whilst retaining overall accuracy is just one approach to historical fiction, however.

Extra characters can be inserted into the historical accounts without doing them violence. After all, history often only records the names of a few notables at great events. The presence of a certain fictional lady-in-waiting, foreign spy or minor nobleman does not make the account of events in the story implausible in the way that having a French army suddenly turn up at Bosworth would do.

Depending on the degree to which a story varies from the historical version, it can be considered pseudo-historical or alternate historical. Pseudo-historical plays, novels and movies are often inaccurate, throwing together people who lived decades apart or altering events in the interest of a good story. This can be misleading to someone who does not know much about the period, and misconceptions

to say how events might have turned out had the Wars of the Roses taken a different course. What if Lord Stanley had joined Richard III at Bosworth Field and contributed to defeating Henry Tudor? What if Henry VI had been executed when he was first captured and a different Lancastrian candidate put forward? What if Richard of Gloucester had escorted his brother's son to London and watched over him as Lord Protector instead of taking his crown?

This makes for some very interesting speculation about the course of later history, but all that can be said with certainty is that British history since the Wars of the Roses proceeds from a set of very particular circumstances. If any of them were changed, the outcome would be greatly different and it is not possible to say what the world we live in today would be like.

History, Fiction and Reimaginings

The Wars of the Roses have inspired a great deal of fiction. Some of it is what can be termed 'straight historical' fiction, i.e. set against the historical narrative, with real people portrayed

arising from a piece of popular entertainment can become 'facts that everyone knows'.

The purpose of pseudo-historical tales is entertainment. There are those that like accurate historical details – and there is much that can be learned about a period of history from accurate or 'straight' historical fiction – but many people just want to be entertained. A general feeling of medieval-ness, a few familiar names, places and so forth will generally suffice.

Shakespeare's plays can be considered to be pseudo-historical. He was writing the Hollywood blockbusters of the day, rather than creating classic literature that would be studied for centuries to come. There were less explosions and convenient use of technology as a plot device,

Above: William Shakespeare's plays were the blockbuster action movies and romantic comedies of the day, played similarly fast and loose with historical reality. Performing for the Tudor dynasty, he was mindful of a need to portray their enemies as villains.

but the principles were the same: heroes and villains, hard choices, tragedy and comedy, and of course excitement. Shakespeare's representations of Richard III, Henry V and so forth have been repeated, reinterpreted and reinvented so many times that they have entered the common consciousness, but that does not mean that they are necessarily accurate.

The portrayal of characters like Henry VII and Richard III in Shakespeare and other fiction was influenced by the culture of the day. At the time that Shakespeare was writing the Tudors ruled England, so vilifying those that had opposed them was probably a sensible option. There was also the necessity of presenting a play with clearly identifiable characters. It might be possible to explore the complex motivations of a character in a novel, but for a play to be entertaining it had to present fairly simple characters that the audience could keep track of.

The same applies to alternate-historical fiction, where some event changes the course of history that we are familiar with. Such tales often involve notable historical characters, who might be portrayed quite realistically or however the author wants them to be. Alternative-historical fiction does not need to conform to reality, although the usual rule is that everything before the great history-changing event tends to be the same, and that would generally include characters.

Historical characters have also appeared in fiction set outside our history. Some science-fiction novels have featured historical characters sent to other worlds or the future. The opposite, where a time traveller finds himself in a past era, falls somewhere between this concept and alternate-historical fiction. The events of the Wars of the Roses have also influenced fiction that makes no pretence of being historically accurate. Many science-fiction and fantasy novels are based on a period of history, to the point where it is possible for a reader who spots the parallel to predict the storyline with remarkable accuracy. Other works are inspired but not directly derivative. Of these, George R. R. Martin's *A Song of Ice and Fire*, televised as *Game of Thrones* is worthy

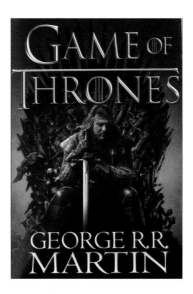

of particular note. *Game of Thrones* is not a direct translation of the Wars of the Roses into a fantasy setting. There would be little point; that story has already been told in numerous history books. It does, however, feature feuding noble houses with strangely familiar-sounding names as well as characters who seem to be parallels to historical people. The basic concept is quite similar – struggle for control of a divided realm, in which treachery and deceit play as great a part as open battle.

Fact or Fiction?

It may be that part of the appeal of such reimaginings or tales inspired by historical events is that they are somewhat familiar. They ring true, because similar events have already happened. Or it may simply be that a good story is always a good story. Whether pure fiction partly inspired by real events, a historical novel woven around real events or a historical narrative describing those events, the Wars of the Roses do indeed make a great story.

This was a highly unpleasant and frightening time to live through, but an important one in terms of its historical outcomes. It remains one of the most fascinating eras for scholars and for those who enjoy historical fiction, and it would appear that the people who lived through those troubled times are still making their presence felt today.

Above: The events of the Wars of the Roses greatly influenced European history… and modern fiction too. *Game of Thrones* **has been a hugely popular TV series shown on HBO. It is derived from George R.R. Martin's** *A Song of Ice and Fire* **that is said to have been inspired by the Wars of the Roses.**

LANCASTER FAMILY TREE

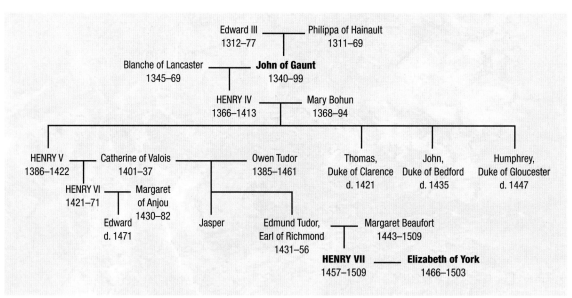

YORK FAMILY TREE

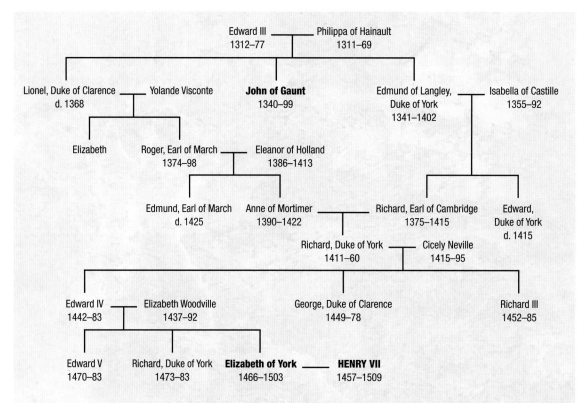

BIBLIOGRAPHY

Baldwin, David. *Stoke Field: The Last Battle of the Wars of the Roses.* Pen and Sword, 2006.

Boardman, Andrew. *The First Battle of St. Albans.* Tempus, 2006.

Bradbury, Jim. *The Routledge Companion to Medieval Warfare.* Routledge, 2004.

Buckley, J A. *Who's Who of the Wars of the Roses.* Penhellick Publications, 2002.

Cheetham, Anthony. *The Wars of the Roses.* Weidenfeld & Nicholson, 2000.

Cook, D R. *Lancastrians and the Yorkists: Wars of the Roses.* Longman, 1984.

Evans, H T. *The Wars of the Roses.* Sutton Publishing, 1998.

Goodman, Anthony. *The Wars of the Roses: The Soldiers' Experience.* Tempus, 2006.

Goodwin, George. *Fatal Colours: the Battle of Towton 1461.* Orion Publishing Group, 2011.

Gravett, Christopher. *Bosworth 1485: The Last Charge of the Plantagenets.* Osprey Publishing, 1999.

Haig, Philip A. *Wakefield & Towton Battlefields: The Wars of the Roses.* Pen & Sword Books, 2002.

Hammond, Peter W. *The Battles of Barnet & Tewkesbury.* Sutton Publishing, 1993

Hicks, Michael. *The Wars of the Roses 1455–1485.* Osprey Publishing, 2003.

Hutton, William. *The Battle of Bosworth Field.* Tempus, 1999.

Ross, Charles. *The Wars of the Roses: A Concise History.* Thames & Hudson, 1976.

Santiuste, David. *Edward IV and the Wars of the Roses.* Pen & Sword, 2010.

Wise, Terence. *The Wars of the Roses.* Osprey Publishing, 1983.

INDEX

PICTURE CREDITS